BEHIND
THE COVER

A Ghostwriter's Guide to Authoring
Your Own Business Book

Write on!

KAREN ROWE

"I'm in the business of helping my clients become published authors. Karen's advice and expertise has proven to be vital in making that happen. If you have a book idea in your head, she can help you get it on paper."

—*Topher Morrison, Bestselling Author*

"A kickass resource for any professional sick to death of spinning their wheels and finally ready to get on and write a book! This was a pleasure to read—it made me laugh out loud and gives great practical guidance. Truly a must-read for leaders, experts, and entrepreneurs."

—*Tina Dietz MS, NSS, Creative Business Expert &*
Audio Publisher

"*Behind the Cover* goes directly to the heart of why authors often fail to achieve the goal of writing a book. Karen provides deep insight into the challenges we face as entrepreneurs and proposes practical yet innovative solutions anyone can benefit from immediately. Whether you've written a book in the past or you're ready to start your first, Karen's book is a must-read!"

—*Trace Kingham, Founder/Chief Experience Officer,*
Kingham Signature Events

"Karen's techniques kept me on track and motivated to move the process forward with ease and grace. I valued her wisdom and expertise while sorting through my own little voice of doubt that often wanted to stop the process. If you apply the information she shares in *Behind the Cover*, you will be absolutely amazed by the results. When you walk away with the first draft of your manuscript, you will be excited beyond belief!"

—*Cathy Yost, Life Coach, Author of* Life Speaks: Challenging Moments Are Our Greatest Gifts

"For the change-agents, creative geniuses, and enlightened gypsies of the world—who have a story and something to offer. Reading this book will propel you into a new possibility for your life and business. Karen Rowe is brilliant at cutting through the overwhelm and showing you how to complete your compelling, bestselling book. You may be the one the world is waiting for. So, what are you waiting for?"

—*Teresa de Grosbois, #1 International Bestselling author of* Mass Influence, *four-time bestselling author, international speaker, and founder of the Evolutionary Business Council*

"If you want to write a non-fiction book, who would you prefer to learn from? Someone that has written a book about how to write a book, or someone that has written more than forty non-fiction books for different industries and has now packaged all her secrets into one easy-to-read resource that you can take action on right now? If you're looking for a new approach to that blank page you've been staring at, *Behind the Cover* is it!"

—*Marc Ensign, Digital marketing strategist, speaker, blogger*

Editorial Project Management: Karen Rowe, www.karenrowe.com
Cover Design: Shake Creative, ShakeTampa.com
Interior Layout: Ljiljana Pavkov

Printed in Canada

ISBN: 978-0-9867638-6-1 (international trade paper edition)
ISBN: 978-0-9867638-7-8 (ebook)

BEHIND
THE COVER

To Craig Howrie,
for standing by me every day
since 1993.

You're the one I speak to
when I need to find my most
authentic voice.
In writing and in life.

"To achieve great things, two things are needed; a plan, and not quite enough time."

—*Leonard Bernstein*

This book has been professionally edited and proofread. However, sometimes typos can slip through the cracks. I believe that done is better than perfect, but I take these typos very seriously. If you find any errors, please email me at **Karen@KarenRowe.com**.

Table of Contents

Foreword by Dan Bradbury

Do you suffer from shiny object syndrome?

I know I do.

Most entrepreneurs love the excitement of doing something new; that's one of the reasons we start our companies in the first place.

Most entrepreneurs also know that one of the best ways to raise their profile and stand out from their competitors is to write and publish their own business book. *Writing* that book, on the other hand, is easier said than done. If you started writing a book but were distracted looking for the shiny, new, exciting option to pour your energy into before you finished it—you're not the only one.

Thousands of people teach how to overcome this block, yet rarely do the students who follow their advice get the results they expect. This is because traditional advice on how to write a book is missing critical pieces of the puzzle, which may keep you struggling for years. To build authority, dominate your niche, and start making tens of thousands of dollars a month, it's important to follow a very specific (yet simple) process, which Karen has clearly outlined in *Behind the Cover: A Ghostwriter's Guide to Authoring Your Own Business Book.*

When I first came to Karen, I was ready to seriously scale my business. I was interested in having a professionally written and published book to raise my profile and use as a core-positioning tool. I had previously published lead magnets and done well with them, but these publications were insufficient for the level at which I was conducting business. I was looking to raise my game. I knew it was time to take my business to the next level, and writing a book was the next step.

I am an investor specializing in taking companies already producing multiple six- figure revenues and accelerating their growth to over £10 million. I started with nothing and built my business from the ground up. In my twenties, I built and sold my first business for over £1Million. At thirty-one, I turned a U.S. company around that was listed on the U.S. Stock Market for $4.3 Million. I have worked with over eight thousand business owners in over sixty-nine different countries worldwide. My company is the number one place for small business owners to get the resources, support, and guidance to systemize and scale their revenue, profit, and time. We teach rapid, profitable growth for your business.

It was obvious I needed a book. I was interested in Karen's process for two reasons: speed and location. I knew if I didn't get my book written in Q1, it wasn't going to get done. From the start, it was clear that Karen was as committed to the success of my book as I was. She is passionate about helping her clients write the very best book possible and making the process as easy as possible. My book, *Breeding Gazelles: Fast Growth Strategies for Your Business*, was published in April 2016 and has better positioned me as an industry leader. The caliber of clients coming through to see us now is much higher.

My experience says that writing a book is not exciting—it's not sexy—but *nothing* will beat well-planned, consistent action. And Karen is the person to help you get results. You will get the technical knowledge you need, along with the practical information and kick in the pants required to get over your excuses and actually finish and publish your book.

Your business is capable of far more than you think it is. Most business owners just don't think big enough. You can't just think big; you need to *do* big. You can't just have the goal; you need to be able to execute that goal. In business, you are only as strong as your weakest link. Does that mean you have to have all of the skills and resources yourself? No. But your company does. If that weak link is in writing or content generation, you need to read this book.

If you have always wanted to author your own business book that will reinforce your authority and expertise in the business world but you don't know where to start, or you're stuck somewhere in the book writing process, *Behind the*

Cover is the book you need to get to the finish line as quickly as possible. Letting yourself get distracted by all those bright, shiny objects is what separates wannabes from successful business owners.

Don't just join in. Jump in.

Dan Bradbury
Founder, Dan Bradbury Ltd.
Author of *Breeding Gazelles: Fast Growth Strategies for Your Business*
Warwickshire, United Kingdom

Thank You

To Topher Morrison, for constantly embarrassing me in public by introducing me as "the rudest Canadian" you've ever met. Thank you for being the one who allows me to live and work in America.

To my fellow Key People of Influence. I am so glad to be a part of this tribe. Thank you to those of you who contributed feedback on content, title, and cover design.

To my clients. I consider it my deep privilege that you let me help you tell your story.

To Colin Theriot, Gabriel Aluisy, Canon Wing, Michael McCoy, and Bruce Serbin. Thank you for allowing me to share your brilliant content.

To Jay Fiset—the day you saw something in me, my whole life changed. I would not be where I am today without you.

To Colin Collard. I'm not sure you'll ever realize how big an impact you have had on my life and my business. I continue to reap the benefits of your contribution to me on a daily basis. Thank you.

To Dave VanHoose, for saying, "Hey, you should move to Tampa!" And to Allyson Giles for making sure I did.

To Teresa de Grosbois. You have taught me everything I know about relationship marketing and have been one of my earliest and most loyal supporters. Thank you.

I learned the art of being a low-maintenance date from Shawne Duperon. Thank you for teaching me how to be with people.

To Mark Katz, for bringing structure and systems to my chaos. And for being the guy perched on my shoulder whispering good deeds in my ear.

To Kelly Oliver. Thank you for helping me to "own my no." And for every laugh along the way.

To Heather Higdon, for standing for me to own my power and greatness.

To Gray Videnka, for being a leader of leaders.

To my coaches: Cathy Yost, for lovingly challenging my deepest assumptions, and eA Cross, for being interested in a fundamental shift in the way I operate in the world.

To Melanie Jones, for being the one who started it all. And for always knowing when to pull the trigger on pie.

To Laurel Lepine, because you were the very first person to ever introduce me as a writer. You are always such a breath of fresh air.

To Laura Crosby and Shanna Corning, my sister-wives, for keeping me alive during some of my stormiest years. For your positivity, sense of humor, fun, and unwavering support. I admire you both beyond words and am so proud to be your friend.

To Echo Gettis, for grace and love and grit. If I lived closer, I'd be on your doorstep with cupcakes and gin all the time.

To my family, Mom, Dad, Ian, Jane, and Sri, for loving me through the rough years as I danced along the border between turbulence and order. Thank you for all you have done to see me through to the other side.

To my editors: Julia Petrisor, for your willingness, always, to show up and jump in with both feet and ask questions later, and to Rebecca Pillsbury for taking my steaming pile of blog posts and webinar and podcast transcripts and turning them into something I am proud to publish.

I have spent the better part of eight years in personal and professional growth and development training. From Personal Best Seminars to the Grow Op to the Evolutionary Business Council, Speaking Empire, Landmark Worldwide, Key Person of Influence and Make Your Mark Speaking and Training. I would not be here without the thousands of hours and countless people who have been part of my journey.

Who I am, and this book I've written, could not have been possible without any of you. Thank you.

Preface:

WHEN IT CAN'T WAIT UNTIL MONDAY

"Procrastination is the thief of time."

—Edward Young

"The quality of your life is in direct proportion to the amount of uncertainty you can comfortably deal with."

—Tony Robbins

t's 11 p.m. on a Friday night, and my phone rings. Unknown number.

If someone is calling at that time of night, it must be urgent.

I answer.

A stranger says, "Hi Karen, my name is Louise. This may sound a bit odd, but I have a powerful need to write a book.

However, I have *no* writing experience and feel I *have* to get this book out to the public soon. But . . . I have no idea how to do this! Would you be able to help me?"

I love calls like this.

She tells me her story.

Earlier that day, she was sitting in the middle of an audience of roughly four hundred people at a business training course. The facilitator was speaking with a woman who had overcome fibromyalgia and was considering writing a book about her experience. But she wasn't sure her book would be any good, and she wondered if it would really make a difference. How should she move forward?

The facilitator asked the audience, "How many of you have fibromyalgia or know someone who does?"

Over half the room raised their hands.

The facilitator turned to the woman and said, "*Every day you don't write your book, you're putting someone else at a disadvantage.*"

Louise was stunned. It felt as if she'd been hit by a bolt of lightning. The facilitator might as well have been speaking directly to her.

She had never considered writing a book before, but she realized in that moment that she, too, had answers to a problem from which many people suffer. Recently, she had suffered a concussion, and after having consulted with more than twenty specialists who had told her there was nothing they could do to speed up her recovery from post-concussion syndrome, she had taken matters into her own hands.

The facilitator shared my name with the room. Louise knew it was late, but she had to call me immediately—it just couldn't wait until Monday.

This is what happens when a client truly connects their message—their "why"—to the urgency of getting a book written. Within a month, Louise was on a plane; she spent three days with me in Florida and got the first draft of her book written. Just like that.

If you're reading this, chances are that you also have specialized knowledge to share. If you had the opportunity to ask a roomful of people how many of them have dealt with or know someone who has dealt with the particular problem you solve, the percentage would astound you.

"How many of you have dealt with struggles in your small business?"

"How many of you have had a hard time writing a book (or know someone who has)?"

"How many of you are single and wish you weren't (or know someone who is)?"

"How many of you struggle with reaching your ideal weight?"

These are just a few examples of questions you might ask.

I never did hear from the woman who had overcome fibromyalgia. I don't know if her book ever got—or ever will get—written. That is the difference between those who take action and those who don't.

What Have You Been Waiting For?

How long have you been talking about writing your book? How long have you been writing it or telling people you're writing it? Do you shudder every time someone asks you, "How's that book coming along?"

You are being stingy. Every day you don't write your book, you are depriving people of your knowledge and experience, of your story and of your message. Every day your book is not out in the world is a day that others don't have the benefit of your brilliance. If you think that what you have to say is nothing special or not brilliant, that is an excuse you use to keep you stuck and to keep you safe. Everyone has a unique perspective from which someone else can benefit. There is someone out there in a great deal of pain—be it physical, emotional, psychological, or spiritual—searching for the information you have learned and possibly mastered but are keeping to yourself.

Sure, but there are already so many other books out there on this topic, you might be thinking. That may be true, but none of them are in *your* voice—the voice that may speak to one particular person. Or one hundred. Or one thousand. Those other books just didn't work for them. Yours will.

This book is your wake-up call. No one's life can be transformed by the book that never got written. *You* have a book to write.

Introduction

> *"Ideas in secret die.*
> *They need light and air,*
> *or they starve to death."*
>
> **—Seth Godin**

Think about a book that has changed your life.

The Four Agreements, The War of Art, The Way of the Superior Man, Eat, Pray, Love, The Wealthy Barber, Women, Food and God, How to Win Friends and Influence People... Books like these have all had a profound and lasting impact on my life.

I have books I refer to again and again, like bibles that enrich my life every time I pick them up. Sometimes, I wonder, *What if those books had never been written?*

Think and Grow Rich was published seven years into the Great Depression. It asserts that desire, faith, and persistence can propel you to great heights if you can suppress negative thoughts and focus on long-term goals. Imagine what a revolutionary book that must have been at the time.

Even now, nearly eighty years after its original publication, it is ranked as the sixth bestselling paperback book of all time. What if *Think and Grow Rich* had never been published?

A book like *The Secret*—although its message may now seem commonplace or might even make you roll your eyes—was a revelation in 2006. It transformed people's relationships with their thoughts and made us realize we had a say in controlling our outcomes and creating the life of our dreams. What if Rhonda Byrne had just said, "Nah. I'm gonna keep this information to myself."

Imagine if no one had helped Stephen R. Covey get his book, *The 7 Habits of Highly Effective People*, to market, or if Jim Collins had let fear prevent him from writing *Good to Great*. If Brené Brown had ignored the call to write *The Gifts of Imperfection* or worried too much that her book would suck and be boring.

There is and always will be a need for books. Although the medium may constantly be evolving—we are shifting at an increasing and sometimes alarming rate into online platforms, one-click purchasing, and seven-second attention spans—that does not change the fact that the thought leaders of our generation have something to say.

We want to learn from their wisdom. We want to learn from *your* wisdom. If you keep that content to yourself, you are doing a great injustice to the planet. And, if you're a bottom-line type of person, it is costing you money—and it is costing you clients. What if your book is the next *The Secret*? Or the next *Good to Great* or the next *Think and Grow Rich*?

> *"The book that changes your life*
> *the most is not a book that you read;*
> *it's the book you write."*

> **—Daniel Priestley**

Daniel Priestley, author of three bestselling books and founder of Dent, a business growth accelerator program, describes the writing process as a journey that is about "tuning out from consumption—tuning out from the noise, tuning out from the endless stream of products coming at you, from the endless stream of books that you could be reading—and moving into creativity mode. . . . This is a big switch from what most of the world does, which is consume, into what very few people are willing to do, which is to create."

This is not to say that writing your book is easy. Moving from consumer to creator is a big leap. Most of us know that the problem with writing a book is . . . *writing* the damn book! It's time-consuming, and it's a chore. As a professional writing coach and ghostwriter, I see this all the time.

Studies have shown[1] that the biggest obstacle to success is simply getting started. We are prone to procrastinating on large projects, focusing instead on the small, mindless tasks that fill up our time. However, if we simply just get started, human nature is also prone to wanting to finish what we start. When you start watching a movie or reading a book, you want to know how it ends, right?

This is what my proven system, Book at the Beach, is all about. Book at the Beach is exactly what it sounds like—the client and I meet in a hotel room at the beach, sit down, and focus on nothing else but their book for three entire days. We start the first draft, and we finish it. I love this method, simply put, because it's fast. I have always been extremely goal-oriented; I do not get a high from "the process" or "the journey," and neither do my clients. I get juice out of producing a result they couldn't get without me—out of capturing genius on a page. I love getting a story out of the client's head and into the reader's hands, where it belongs.

Like many of you, I went through a phase where getting my knowledge and experience on the page was a ridiculous struggle. Okay, I'll be honest—I still struggle to stay motivated at times, but thankfully, whenever I get stuck now, I have a proven method to refer to that gets me back on track. And I will be sharing it with you for the first time ever, in this book.

My Secret Superpower (You Have It, Too!)

The first book I ever wrote was finished in less than six weeks. Sounds incredible, and it was. Less than a year later, a mentor pointed out that writing a book in such a short amount of time was a superpower, and that I should build a business around it. So I did—but at the time, I didn't know what that superpower actually *was*, let alone how to teach it.

In the first few years of my business, I struggled to help my clients successfully finish their books and get them published. It was very frustrating. Being goal-oriented, I wanted to feel the pleasure and glory of completion. And, more importantly, I wanted my clients to feel that, too. I wanted them to feel the rush of becoming a published author, the satisfaction of a job well done, the thrill of seeing their name on Amazon, and the overwhelming joy of holding the proof copy of their book in their hands for the very first time.

After two frustrating years of coaching, I finally decoded my superpower: I can write a book in three days. In the pages that follow, I outline my method and show you how to connect with your target audience, how to write an outline in record time, how to tell a powerful story, and how to finish your book without wanting to throw yourself off a bridge in the process.

Writing a book is a lot of work, absolutely. But I guarantee that you're making it harder than it needs to be and taking more time than necessary. Follow the steps in the chapters in this book, and I promise you—you'll discover that the process doesn't have to be so painful. A book is your shot at making a difference, at greatness; it is an opportunity to reach immortality. So, there is no time to waste.

Chapter 1:

THE SENSORY DEPRIVATION TANK

My journey as an author began with absolutely no plan in place. I left a secure, tenured teaching position with one goal in mind: *I'm going to be a writer.* I immediately accepted an unpaid position blogging for my local newspaper's website. Within six months, an editor I'd been working with for the blog called with an offer from a publishing company. They were looking for a writer to write a book on chocolate. Was I interested?

Am I interested?!

Do I want to win the lottery and move to Paris? Heck yes, I'm interested! It paid $4,000. I felt like I had hit the jackpot.

But all the romantic visions I ever had of writing were blown out of the water the first time I sat down to actually write a book. After the first few weeks of elation had worn off—the satisfaction of having left teaching, the triumph of quitting my day job to write full time, the exhilaration of cashing my first check, the euphoria from having a real, live publisher reach out to little ole' me?—*there was work to do.*

I had to deliver a 45,000-word manuscript and had only eight weeks in which to do it. That meant I had to write roughly a thousand words a day. Sounds easy, right? And it would have been, had I gotten started straight away. But I didn't.

First, I took a vacation for two weeks. I was arrogant and naïve—foolish enough to believe that the hardest part of writing a book (getting the book deal and being picked up by a publisher) was behind me. Ha! I gallivanted off to Belize as if the book were a foregone conclusion.

It wasn't, of course.

I returned from my trip and spent two weeks "doing research," which, in my case, meant surfing the Internet, copying and pasting things that I thought were "neat," and plowing my way through some peanut butter cups. Yup. *I was a writer.*

So now, I was down to four weeks left, and not one real word had been written. It was then that I realized something serious had to be done. I was completely unprepared for how hard the writing process would be—and not even the *writing* part. The rest of it. The resistance, the self-sabotage, the insecurity, the paralyzing fear—of success, of failure, of performance, and of my ability to deliver.

I had to acknowledge how scared I was. I had to take action. Something drastic. I had to leave town. I had to physically remove myself from the comforts of my home and disappear to a cabin in the middle of nowhere for six days. I mean, how cliché can you get?

There was no Internet, no TV, and no cell phone reception. No Facebook, no friends to talk to, *there wasn't even any running water*. This place was completely devoid of any and all distractions. Perfect. It was exactly what I needed. I called it my Sensory Deprivation Tank. It was so remote that it didn't even have a mailing address; the owners had to send me a hand-drawn map and a picture of the front of the house so I could find it. That was when the rubber hit the road.

One of the things no one ever tells you about writing a book is how lonely and isolating it is. I went down a rabbit hole without fully knowing what I was in for. As an extrovert, those were six of the longest, darkest, loneliest, scariest, crazy-making days of my life. It felt like I was starring in my own personal *Blair Witch Project*. It was intensely painful. These were the front lines. I sat in front of my computer for twelve to fourteen hours a day, sometimes longer. I was doing battle.

This wasn't how I thought it was going to be. Visions of quiet tables in quaint cafés in Paris à la Hemingway were annihilated. Where were the shenanigans? The love affairs? The *chocolate croissants*? I was not surrounded by Gertrude Stein or Picasso or the Eiffel fucking Tower. I was surrounded by nothing and nobody but my own thoughts. It was less "sexy *café* à *Paris*," more "punishing penitentiary."

3

I was in a town of 140 people in the Badlands of Alberta. Where was *my* Moveable Feast?

All I wanted to do was get the hell out of there. I would stare longingly at my car and think, *All I have to do is get in and drive away.* Back to civilization and back to my life. But I had a deadline, and not having any distractions was exactly what I needed. It was awful . . . and it worked.

I can't describe the experience as anything other than traumatic. I woke up, I ate breakfast, I wrote. I ate lunch, I wrote. I ate dinner. I wrote, I wrote, I wrote, I went to bed. I wrote from fear and panic; I wrote, uncertain if I could do it; I wrote, not knowing at all if I was making a horrible mistake. I wrote, worried that I wasn't good enough, smart enough, or disciplined enough to pull it off. I wrote, mostly, so I could get the hell out of there and go back home. I typed so much over the course of those six days that my knuckles got sore.

Finally, I couldn't take it anymore. With the most dire case of cabin fever, I came back two days earlier than planned, fleeing that small ghost town like it was the scene of a crime. In fact, it was. It was stark and lonely and harrowing. (At least, it felt that way to me at the time.) I had been my own slave driver. It was just me and the material. I was so desperate for human contact, but I closed my eyes, held my breath, and barreled on through to the finish line. It was a cage match to the death.

Years later, I found out this was a completely normal part of the process. This is, in fact, what it means to be a writer. It is the creative process. It is what Steven Pressfield calls

"The Muse," but I didn't know that at the time. I just felt like a lunatic. That being said, it also felt more like *me* than anything I'd ever done in the past. Yes, I was out in the middle of no-where . . . an alien, in a place I didn't belong; yet strangely, I belonged there more than I ever had in the classroom.

Without ever realizing it, I had spent six years of my life as a teacher feeling like a fraud. This first book was about me stepping into my own and feeling, deep in my bones, that, *Yes! This is what I'm meant to be doing.* I had never felt more complete, more like myself, or more centered, calm, or focused—amid the stark-raving panic, I mean. But for the most part, I felt grateful for having discovered this truth about myself relatively early on in my life. I was thirty-four at the time. Thank God I hadn't wasted twenty more years of my life wasting away in a middle school classroom, watch-ing the life slowly leak out of me. But that didn't make the actual writing—the sitting down and coming face-to-face with every fear I had ever had in my entire life—any less excruciating.

Those six days took years off my life, but I wrote more than ten thousand words and laid a solid foundation for my book. I had messed around for so long that, in the end, I had left myself only eight days to complete twenty-five thou-sand words. I was averaging about ten thousand words per week. I'm not good at math, but I was pretty sure that meant I was running out of time.

I called my publisher to renegotiate a later deadline. Much to my astonishment, she said no.

This sucker had to be pounded out in time for Valentine's Day, which meant my October 1 deadline was firm and final. What I also didn't know was that there was an entire team of people waiting for *me* to finish. Delaying by a few weeks or even a few days would throw off the entire production schedule.

Oh.

This was real.

There was no getting out of this.

It mattered if I finished.

People were counting on me.

Up until that point, I had been treating the deadline like a suggestion. Now, I had created a crisis. I had to write twenty-five thousand words in eight days. It seemed impossible. But this non-negotiable, external deadline that I had left to the very last minute left me with no other choice. So, I did the only thing there was left to do:

I wrote like my life depended on it.

I wrote like there was a gun to my head.

It was a race to the finish. It took everything I had in me. On more than one occasion, I thought, *There is no way.* But here is the great thing about a deadline that's so tight: *There is no time for your own bullshit.* All there's time for is more typing, eating with one hand, and maybe some low-grade mouth-breathing.

I created a new mantra: *There is always a way.* In those eight days, I learned more about writing and more about myself than ever before. *There is always a way.* I grew up in

6

those eight days. *There is always a way.* I became a writer in those eight days.

My experience of myself was completely transformed.

That deadline was the best thing that ever happened to me.

The Lesson

Writing a book—I imagine—is a little like giving birth; you forget all about the pain when this beautiful thing comes rushing into the world. The struggle seems completely worth it. Once you get that book in your hands, once people get to read the words you wrote and get impacted by you sharing your story . . . well, you forget about doing all the work while crying.

And after my first book deal, I got a second book deal. I did it all over again. My return to the Sensory Deprivation Tank for my second book was reluctant, inevitable . . . and surprisingly lovely. Mostly, I felt free—unencumbered from the crushing responsibility of my day-to-day life.

By then, I was all-in with my freelance writing career. Translation: *I was broke.* Going out to the Sensory Deprivation Tank became a reprieve from the stress of supporting myself through my art. *All I have to do is write.* I didn't have to talk to anybody, explain myself, say no, say thank you, say sorry, shower, brush my teeth, or worry about income, which was a major preoccupation for me by then.

All I had to do was write.

The first time, it had felt like a prison; the second time, it felt like a warm cocoon. Just another reminder that situations are what you make of them.

My eternal lesson: *Suffering is optional.*

I didn't want to leave that second time. I wanted to stay in that false reality longer. But the real world would not wait. The real world was impatient and needed to be paid. The real world had a return call to make and emails to answer. I returned home after a week, once again with a solid foundation, a habit created, and a fresh perspective.

My Proven System

When I first started coaching people on how to finish and publish their own books, my clients' book projects would inevitably get stalled; months and months and months would pass with no progress. I was stumped. *Why don't they just sit down and write?!*

Well. That's like asking someone who wants to lose weight why they don't just get on a treadmill and go for a run. They want the end result, but they don't necessarily want to do the hard work required to get them there. Or they are letting their fear run the show.

Not everyone is willing or able to go into sensory deprivation mode. I admit, it can be a horrible place. It's the least sexy thing ever. The reason my clients hired me in the first place was specifically so they didn't have to deal with any pain. Like everyone, they wanted a bypass. A quick fix. A magic bullet. And I didn't have one.

Not yet, anyway.

I was focusing on *how* to write a book when what I should have been doing was focusing on how to *bypass* the part everyone hates—the hideous, dreadful book-writing process. Can we get to the end without having to enter the mouth of the lion, slay the dragon, kill the beast?

Turns out, you totally can.

The remainder of this book will lay out the steps and strategies that make it possible for me—and my clients—to successfully complete a book in record time, without all the suffering. You will be led through the same guidelines I use with my clients—how to determine your book's niche, develop an Ideal Reader Profile, follow a Rapid Results Outline, and use a blueprint to create your initial draft. You will learn how to uncover your unique voice, use storytelling as a tool to connect with your target audience, and how to use mind tricks to get your book done even faster. Once you've knocked out your first draft, I offer unique self-editing strategies for you to conduct before I teach you how to hire a stellar team of professional editors, designers, and maybe even a ghostwriter (in case your first draft didn't quite go as planned). Finally, I clarify the process for publishing your book, and I offer a bonus chapter on writing a kick-ass foreword.

If the thought of writing your book makes you want to run screaming from the room or curl up in the fetal position, then you are in the right place. Read on.

Chapter 2

SHIT OR GET OFF THE POT

"If somebody offers you an amazing opportunity but you are not sure you can do it, say yes—then learn how to do it later."

—Richard Branson

It wasn't until four years into my new business that I stumbled quite accidentally upon my signature offering: the one that truly led me to discover the secrets I am going to share in this book. I moved from Alberta, Canada to Tampa, Florida in 2013, and I was unprepared in every way—emotionally, mentally, spiritually, and physically. And yet, in some ways, it was perfect.

Although it took some time, everything worked out as it was meant to: I met the right people at the right time and began growing my business in a very natural way. I secured several high-end clients, one of whom was a successful seven-figure entrepreneur. As you might expect, scheduling interviews with a high-powered, alpha-male executive was not the easiest thing to do. Even doing ninety-minute sessions once a week put us at a timeline that made it impossible to get his book out by the date he wanted; at that rate, it would have taken a minimum of six months just to get the first draft written.

Here was a client who wanted his book done and done yesterday. As we were looking for time in our already-packed schedules, he asked, "What if I rent us two hotel rooms at the beach and we knock this thing out in three or four days. Can you do it?"

Without skipping a beat, I said yes.

Then, all the air left my body. I couldn't breathe.

We set a date, and I calmly hung up the phone as if I had done this a million times.

And then I completely fell apart. *Amygdala hijack.* Because I didn't actually know if I could do it. My heart was racing, the sky was falling, and I was pretty sure that the apocalypse was about to arrive at any second. I phoned my business coach in a panic and bleated frantically into the phone, "*I just said I would write a book in three days, and I don't know if I can deliver on that promise!*"

I thought he was going to say, "Are you crazy?? Call that man back and get out of it, *as soon as possible*."

This is the reason we have business coaches, people. For times like this. Because that's not what he said.

He said, (much more rationally, I might add), "Relax. You already have a system. All we need to do is figure out exactly what needs to take place in those three days so that he can walk out with the first draft of his book."

I think he may even have laughed ~~at~~ with me. Then he helped me figure it out.

He even came up with the name: Book at the Beach.

Damn, that was sexy. Much sexier than Sensory Deprivation Tank, am I right?

Say Yes First

Tina Fey is credited with saying, "Say 'yes,' and you'll figure it out afterwards." That, in a nutshell, is the genesis of the Book at the Beach, the single greatest offering I have in my business to date. An opportunity presented itself, and in that split second before there was time to think about it, talk myself out of it, rationalize, be practical, or "mull it over," I went for it. You can do the same with your book. Just say yes. Swing for the fences.

It may feel impractical, crazy, reckless, inconvenient, or downright dangerous. That's how you know you're onto something. If you have an immediate and overwhelming impulse to run, if your entire body heaves with fear, and if your first thought is, *Oh, hell no*, it's a definite sign that you should do that very thing. That impulse is your soul speaking to you. And the overwhelming emotional response is your fear on loudspeaker; your identity is just doing its job—protecting itself, protecting you, and maintaining the status quo. It will feel like a threat because, to your identity, *it is a threat*. That is the whole point. The reaction will be out of proportion to the stimulus because it has triggered the identity's need for protection.

Ignore that shit.

The amygdala (or the identity or the ego or whatever you want to call it) is part of our primitive brain, designed to keep us safe from saber-toothed tigers and woolly mammoths when we were cavemen and cavewomen. The brain doesn't know the difference between a real threat (you are actually in physical danger and being chased by a lion) and a perceived threat (writing your book and sharing your personal narrative with the world). One will kill you, the other will just *feel* like it is killing you. Big difference.

You have to ignore the fight-or-flight instinct and forge ahead. This is, in fact, what I was dealing with in those days in the Sensory Deprivation Tank and in the weeks that preceded my deadline. The rewards for forging ahead will exceed your wildest expectations. This is the path—and, dare I say it, the only path—to getting your book written.

Why You Aren't Writing Your Book

> *"Fears unfaced become your limits."*
>
> **—Robin Sharma**

Once you say "yes," it involves committing to that yes over and over again until the book is done. In other words, you have to set and keep a deadline. No matter what. Your brain will seek out every excuse in the book (ahem) *not* to do this. As long as you are giving more power to those excuses, your book will never get written, and you will be in exactly this same spot a year from now.

Ultimately, knowing *why* your book isn't getting written has no bearing on finishing it. That said, knowing why may help you break a pattern of incompletion to see your way through to the antidote—or action—required. So here are some of the biggest excuses people use to stall on their books:

1. Time
2. Money
3. Fear
4. I Don't Know How (to Write a Book)
5. I Don't Know Why (I Want to Write a Book)

Time & Money

"I'm too busy."

"As soon as [insert best excuse you have—*this project is complete; the baby is born; the kids are back in school; I am feeling better; Christmas is over, etc.*], I will be able to focus more on the book."

"As soon as I land this next big client, I will have the money."

Used one of those lines before? Well, they make about as much sense as saying, "Writing my book is threatening to destroy the space-time continuum" or "I can't write the

15

book because there is milk in the fridge." There is absolutely no correlation between not working on your book and the reason you're not working on your book. Here's the hard truth—time and money are not even real excuses. They are convenient and lazy considerations masquerading as excuses. They can both be overcome with prioritization.

> There is an ancient Chinese proverb that says, "The best time to plant a tree was twenty years ago. The second-best time is now." The same goes for a book. The best time to start writing your book was probably last year or last month or last week. The second-best time is right now.

Fear

Most of the time, when a client comes to me and has been stalled on their book for a long period of time, it's because they are afraid. They may not see it. They may think it's because they've been busy or because of one of the other excuses I just wrote about, but usually, fear is at the core of those excuses. Maybe you don't believe you can write a book, or you worry that the content you have isn't any good. Fear is part of the process—push through it. If you're not a natural writer but you're a natural speaker, you can either hire someone else to do the writing or record yourself speaking and have it transcribed (more on these options later in this chapter and in Chapter 10).

I Don't Know How (to Write a Book)

The passion you have for your book idea doesn't translate onto the page. You have so much to say, but as soon as you sit down to write, you draw a blank. This is the infamous "writer's block" we've all heard about and that every writer experiences at some time or another. Thankfully, there are numerous strategies that can be used to overcome this problem—including the tried-and-true method I use with my clients and will share with you in future chapters.

I Don't Know Why (I Want to Write a Book)

Maybe you're not writing because you don't have a big enough reason *why* you want to do it. Do you know your reason why? You need to be clear on your why—your burning desire, your big payoff for doing what you do.

If you are a business owner, you understand that—when done properly—a book is a tool to help you increase your reach, establish your credibility, and sustainably grow your business to outrageous levels of success. Writing a book is a game changer for your business. Books work because you get tremendous insight into your business, your philosophy, your systems and process, and your product offering. Your pitch changes. Books generate speaking gigs and press inquiries. A book is the single fastest way to deliver a message and to deliver it in your absence.

> "I like to imagine that each book is like a little ambassador who goes out and meets people. Each book tells your story perfectly each time, it never gets tired or sick, and it goes directly to wherever people want to meet (sometimes in the bath)."
>
> **—Daniel Priestley**

Maybe your burning desire is instead to create a family heirloom—a memoir or family history that can be passed down for generations. Maybe you've had a particular experience or hold wisdom that you know will serve others—you feel a calling to get it out to the world. Or, like my client, Louise, you realize that every day you don't write your book, you are robbing someone else of your genius. There are numerous reasons to write a book; know and understand your deepest reason why, and then get to work, because that *why* will keep you committed and keep you on track when you need it the most.

The Natural Laws of Completion

There comes a time in every wannabe writer's life that, directly put, you've got to shit or get off the pot.

If you've been procrastinating for years on writing your book, maybe it's just not meant to be written—at least not by you, not right now. Either way, you have to decide: Are you going to do this thing or not?

Recently, I took on finishing a project that I had been putting off for over a year. My mantra: *publish or perish*. Total number of actual hours worked to get it to the next phase? Fifteen. Total cost to me in added stress, anxiety, worry, sleepless nights, and lost revenue from other projects over the past year? Countless.

The work that was required was cumbersome and messy and was as tedious as I thought it was going to be. *But*—it didn't take anywhere near as long as I thought it would. In my head, I had built it up to be this insurmountable, never-ending, impossible task that had two heads and breathed fire. And it was only cumbersome and messy and tedious because I had left it so long.

> "The work you do while you procrastinate is probably the work you should be doing for the rest of your life."
>
> **—Jessica Hische**

I used this lesson to help my clients. If you are stuck, break down a task that may seem insurmountable into manageable tasks. My mentor, Topher Morrison, helped me to understand how to do this most effectively by explaining the "Natural Laws of Completion."

Natural Law #1

Incompletions drain and suck energy away from your mind, body, and soul. If you have something incomplete in your life, every time you think about it, it zaps your energy. If I've got something on my task list that I'm avoiding, every single time I look at it and it's incomplete, I think, *I can't do that today*. But really, it's because I don't have the energy.

Natural Law #2

Completions give energy to our mind, body, and soul. They light us up. You have probably had times when you got nothing done all day but you worked your ass off. Then you got home and were too tired to even cook because nothing was accomplished that day. Conversely, you've probably also had days where you crushed it. You got everything on your list done, one after another, and you got home and had the energy to work even longer. It's because your day had completions.

How These Laws Pertain to Your Book

How do we use these two natural laws, which seem to oppose one another? The key to getting energy back into your life as an entrepreneur, a business owner, or a book writer is to make sure you have more completions than incompletions by the end of the day.

There are four ways to score a completion on something.

Option #1: Complete It

It's pretty basic. Suck it up, put on your Adulting pants, and go out and do the things you know you need to do. Those are the items on your task lists that should be done, could be done, can be done. Just get them done. Suck it up and do it.

We like to think that sometimes we should start with the most important things and work our way down. But often, the most important things are the hardest to get done. I'll give you an example. On my task list every day, I have: gratitude journal, meditation, and planning in solitude. Those are three things I can get done before I start my work day. I schedule twenty-one minutes to meditate, set my timer, and read a passage from one of my favorite poets to set the tone and focus for the day and keep me centered. Easy. I gift myself a completion by planning my day. I'm already winning, and it's not even 8 a.m.

Completing one task may involve breaking the task down into smaller, more manageable chunks. "Today, my job is to get twenty pages of my book complete." If twenty pages seems overwhelming, then break it down to a number you can manage. Ten pages or, heck, how about two? Anything you can do to keep moving the needle forward. I would rather my client get two pages of a chapter done and feel great about it than get nothing done at all.

Option #2: Schedule a Time to Complete It

Schedule a time to complete it, and then put it out of sight, out of mind. This does require a little bit of organization. It requires that you have a system involved to make sure the tasks get done. If you see something that you know you need to do but you're not going to have time to get it done today, don't leave it on your list; it will be an incompletion. Instead, plan for it on a specific day to pop back up on your calendar.

One of the greatest gifts my mentor ever gave me was teaching me to master my calendar. If there is something that I schedule to do later, I put the date in my day-planning system, and it disappears from my task list, so I don't have to see that incompletion glaring at me in the face all day long, sucking the very energy out of my body. Note—there's a difference between scheduling a time to do something and procrastinating. This is not procrastination; it's a strategy to get more accomplished and feel good about it.

Option #3: Declare It Complete

Probably one of the most effective options for entrepreneurs: Simply declare something as complete. "This is complete as it is. I'm never going to do it. The end." If something's been on your task list for more than three or four weeks, chances are it's not as important as you think it is. And it's obviously not urgent. As an entrepreneur (and an author), we have to make some sacrifices to realize that there are things that we just don't get done in life. Instead of leaving them on your list to feel bad about, accept that you are never going to do them, check them off the list, and move on. Is there a Business Journal article sitting on your desk that you keep meaning to read? Throw it the hell away and go, "It's complete. I deem thee complete." You'll be surprised how it frees up your energy.

Start writing your book or let it go and feel good about it. And if you know that you want a book but don't want to do the work, then read on. I have plenty of suggestions for how to take the sting out of writing.

Option #4: Hire Someone to Complete It

If you're convinced you *do* have a book inside of you that needs to get out now—but you truly don't have the time or desire to write it yourself—you may find hiring a ghost-writer to be your best option. Ghostwriting is a common and accepted practice. Almost 40 percent of books on the market today have been ghostwritten. I provide a detailed explanation on hiring the right ghostwriters and editors in Chapter 10.

Complete it. Schedule a time to complete it. Deem it or declare it complete. Or—deem it complete for you and hire a professional or pass it off to someone else to complete. No matter what you decide, take an action right now. *Any action.*

Chapter 3:

IT HARDLY EVER GOES AS PLANNED (BUT YOU STILL NEED A PLAN)

"Plans are of little importance,
but planning is essential."

—Winston Churchill

Start with the End in Mind

I know, you're probably thinking, "But Karen, I haven't even figured out *what* I'm going to write about. I'm not ready to wrap my brain around the launch yet." But you want your book to be read, right? If you don't start with the end in mind, no one will know about your book when it comes time to launch. All that hard work won't have the sweet payoff you are hoping for. The very first question you need to ask yourself is, "How am I going to make money from my book?"

Hardly anything goes as planned anyway, so don't stress about figuring it all out right now or having to stick to your original plan. Having a strategy, however, is the secret sauce that is going to set your book apart from the thousands of other first-time author releases out there.

One of the most successful examples I have ever seen of an author keeping the end in mind was my client Dan Bradbury. Dan is an investor and turnaround specialist with an expertise in taking companies from multiple six-figure revenues to over ten million. He set the date for an event, but rather than sell tickets, he sold copies of his book. To attend the event, participants had to purchase three books for general admission or five books for V.I.P. admission. He had 1,200 books presold before we had even finished the book! Nothing motivates a team like a non-negotiable, external deadline.

Grow Your Platform—Put Gas in Your Car

Dan's book launch was so successful because he has one of the finest and brightest marketing minds around. And he understood one key concept: The key to having a successful book launch—and having readers lined up to buy your book and tell all their friends about it—is having a strong platform. He had developed a well-curated and strong list.

He provided value to that list and had the success rate to prove it. His audience cared about what he had to say, respected him greatly, and happily bought his books for the privilege to be able to attend his event.

Start working on your platform well before your book is ready to launch. Perhaps you already have a substantial network built around your business. That's great! But keep growing it. Tell them about your upcoming book. Build anticipation.

If you're unfamiliar with the term "author platform," in short, it is your ability to reach an audience. It's the size of your email newsletter list, the number of blog subscribers you have, your website traffic, the number of speaking engagements you have lined up, podcast appearances, and so on.

QUESTIONS TO ASK:

▶ What communities are you a part of?
▶ How many of them will support your work?
▶ Are you aligned with key people of influence who will support your book?

Writing a book without a platform is like buying a car and not putting gas in it. You need both to propel the vehicle forward. If you want high-octane, high-performance gas in your vehicle, start with your launch in mind from the beginning—before you even start writing your book.

You need time to build or identify gaps in your platform. Be clear on which strategies you're going to use to get your book out. Here is a short list of ways to build your platform:

- Tele-summits
- Campaign partners
- Blogging
- Social media
- List building (finding new followers)
- Video book trailers
- Online media kits
- Online media tours
- Virtual blog tours
- Podcasting/guesting on other podcasts
- Media appearances

There are many moving parts to a strong and well-built book campaign. If your end goal is to get picked up by a traditional publisher, they will be looking at the strength of your platform.

Decide on a Budget

If you are launching your book without the support of a publisher, you need to devise a budget for your writing, editing, design, publishing, and marketing strategies.

You must be willing and prepared to invest in your book. Uninformed business owners sometimes think that being an author doesn't require an investment. This is mostly because they're not yet clear on how to generate energy around that book and get a return on that investment or have the book work for them as a marketing tool. Decide on your investment and then ask yourself: *How much money am I willing to lose?*

Yep, you read that right. You may earn your money back in book sales, but chances are, you won't. It's impossible to predict how any book will do, so make an investment that you are prepared to lose if things don't go as you'd hoped. It's the same as any other product you have in your business; its success depends on the strength of the marketing.

To be successful, get interested in how to get the book working for you, rather than you working for it. Focus first on putting together a quality book that you are proud to sell, which represents you fully and is a contribution to others. Then focus on how to make a return on that investment. A well-targeted, well-planned, and well-executed marketing plan is the most effective way to have a successful book.

Set a Launch Date: Then Double It and Add Three Months

Pick a launch date for your book and work backwards. Note that your book or creative project won't look the way you think. It will take longer and cost more. Often our expectations don't match the end product. My first business coach would tell me, "Set a date, then double it and add three months." More times than not, that was a much more accurate goal for completing a project. Be realistic with your timeframes.

After the writing and editing, the next step is pre-production (which includes title, cover design, interior layout (book design and typesetting), assigning ISBN and barcode. Publishing is the last step.

In terms of a timeline, I allot three to six weeks to write the first draft, but be realistic. What is going to work for you, given all your existing commitments? Allot three to six months if that will have you be successful, three months for the pre-production and a minimum of six months for the launch. There is overlap for each phase, and you can birth a book from beginning to end in nine months.

Of course, it can be done in less time; if you focus exclusively on the book and nothing else, or if you hire someone, it can take three months or less. It's a matter of what choices you make. Here are some tips to help you determine the timeline for your book.

The average book takes four hundred hours to complete. Plan approximately two hundred hours for the writing and editing and the rest for the "other stuff"—formatting, publishing, marketing, launch, and so on.

The amount of time you'll need to set aside on a regular basis depends on your schedule, your goals, and how much help you will be enlisting. For example, if you can clear your schedule and dedicate yourself full-time to your book, you could have the bulk of it complete in thirty days.

If you can't stretch to that, then what would it look like to dedicate time every day, or one day a week, or two blocks of time twice a week? Add up the hours. What is that going to look like over the course of, say, 90 days or 18 months? If you write six hours a week, you're looking at spending thirteen months, or a little over a year to finish your book. I have some clients who are happy with that because it won't cause a big disruption to their work or family life. I have other clients that want it done *now*. If that is the case, my 5 Steps to Publish is probably a fit for you. This outlines all the steps to get a book in hand in 12 weeks.

5 Steps to Publish

You can get your book done from start to finish in 12 weeks if you follow what I call my 5 Steps to Publish, stay committed and take consistent action. Once you are clear how you are going to make money, have created a budget and set your launch date, the next two steps are to complete the Ideal Reader profile (which I will discuss in Chapter 4) and finish the Rapid Results Outline, which I will discuss in Chapter 5.

Allocate three weeks for the writing (Step 2) and six weeks Editing (Step 3) and three weeks for Step 4, pre-production. This can be done in tandem with Step 3. Finally, Step 5 can be completed in two weeks and includes opening a publisher's account and the file review process.

Regardless of the timeline you choose, be clear from the beginning about what you want, your business goals, and how a book is going to fit within those goals. What will work *realistically* with your schedule? The schedule you create needs to be manageable, attainable, and non-negotiable.

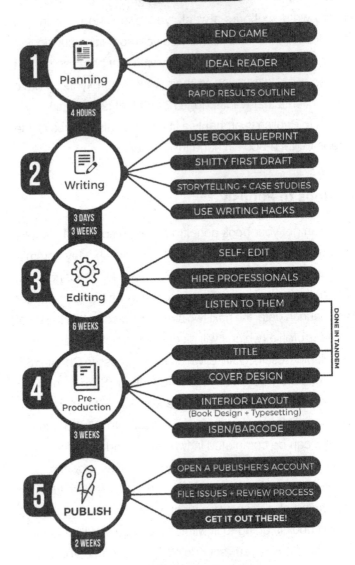

5 STEPS TO PUBLISH

1 Planning — 4 HOURS
- END GAME
- IDEAL READER
- RAPID RESULTS OUTLINE

2 Writing — 3 DAYS - 3 WEEKS
- USE BOOK BLUEPRINT
- SHITTY FIRST DRAFT
- STORYTELLING + CASE STUDIES
- USE WRITING HACKS

3 Editing — 6 WEEKS
- SELF-EDIT
- HIRE PROFESSIONALS
- LISTEN TO THEM

DONE IN TANDEM

4 Pre-Production — 3 WEEKS
- TITLE
- COVER DESIGN
- INTERIOR LAYOUT (Book Design + Typesetting)
- ISBN/BARCODE

5 PUBLISH — 2 WEEKS
- OPEN A PUBLISHER'S ACCOUNT
- FILE ISSUES + REVIEW PROCESS
- GET IT OUT THERE!

TOTAL: 12 WEEKS

Remember, we are focused on results and success, not a half-finished book.

> **Bonus resource:**
> To gain access to my *30 Days to Freedom Action Plan*, head to
> **www.KarenRowe.com/book-bonus**

Ask Yourself These Questions:

1. In a perfect world, what would your ideal *publish* date be?

2. Given your existing commitments, how much time do you have to contribute to your book per week?

3. Do you prefer to be given tasks all at once/at the start of the month, or broken down one task at a time?

4. When you picture yourself working on your book, do you foresee scheduling specific, set times to work on the book and submitting that content at the end of those sessions? Or do you need to meet weekly with a professional in order to complete that work? (In other words, how self-directed are you? Can you be counted on—if given a task—to complete that task, or do you need external accountability?)

Creating a non-negotiable situation (setting a launch date, putting dollars down on an event space, committing a date to your sponsors or clients) will set you up for success. Balance all these considerations against what your time is worth. And if you already know you don't have the time to do all of this, or you don't trust yourself to meet that timeframe, that's why I have a business. Visit www.KarenRowe.com to set up an initial consultation or for access to many of the online resources I have made available.

Chapter 4:

DEFINE YOUR IDEAL READER

You're walking through a bookstore and you stop dead in your tracks. A book cover catches your eye. The title jumps out at you. You can't help but pick it up and flip it over. You're hooked.

This is the power of having a clearly defined Ideal Reader Profile. Before I ever get started with any of my clients, our first step is to figure out who they will be writing to. Even before you define your message, knowing your ideal reader will help you decide what content to write and which message to deliver.

First and foremost, your book content needs to be relevant to your target reader. To achieve that, you need to get a clear picture of exactly who is reading your work. In other words, who is your core audience? In the business world, we call this our "target" or our "ideal client" or our "avatar." I call it your ideal reader. I like to have my client visualize the scenario of his or her book on an endcap in a bookstore (or trolling around on Amazon). An ideal reader is walking (or surfing) by and is so compelled by your book that he or she crosses the bookstore to come over to the shelf and pick it up (or click the button to buy).

Who is that person? How are we going to get them to pick up the book, and how are we going to get them to keep reading? Start by listing possible types of people and niche groups who could be most interested in your book and/or promoting your book, types of people who might like your book, and key people of influence.

Who is Your Perfect Reader?

When I was doing the second edit for one of my books, I made the difficult decision of removing my entire opening story. It was the cornerstone of my book, but *I was writing it for the wrong audience*. It had to go.

I wasted some valuable time by forgetting who I was writing to. Don't make the same mistake I did. Determine now: Who is your target market? More specifically, who is (or who could be) your "perfect reader?" Give us a clear profile and description. Be specific. The clearer you get about your target reader, the easier it will be to write to him or her, and the more your work will resonate the reader—and the more copies of your work will sell. Supply as much detail as you can in this area, such as:

Demographics (e.g., age, gender, employment, income, etc.)

Geographics (e.g., country, state, city, etc.)

Psychographics (e.g., interests, culture, lifestyle, hobbies, buying history, associations they belong to, etc.)

Charity (i.e., where they are spending their money)

Technographics (e.g., customer owns PC; technology enthusiast or pessimist; reads emails and surfs the web [how often, how many hours/week]; uses the web for work, pleasure, or shopping; has bought online before [if so, what product and from where]; websites they visited, etc.)

Start out with general characteristics, such as male between the ages of thirty-five and fifty years old, living in North America, married with two children. Then distil that down. Who would be your *dream client*? Get clear and specific about who is reading. We want that person to have a name, a face, a real physical description. We want them to be nodding while they read your book. Pretend they are sitting across from you. If you have a Facebook fan page, this is a good place to start to get an idea of who your demographic may be. Do this now:

Ideal Reader Profile

1. Sex:
2. Age:
3. Occupation:
4. Income:
5. Education:
6. City, State, Country:
7. Physical description/General appearance:
   a. Height:
   b. Weight:
8. Interests:
9. Culture:
10. Lifestyle:
11. Hobbies:
12. Buying history:
13. Associations he or she belongs to:
14. Technographics:
15. What is their most important asset? (Time, money, loyalty, etc.)
16. What is this person's name?
17. Draw or find a picture of this person.

The final three questions are the most relevant of this entire activity.

18. What is bothering this person right now? What is causing him or her pain?
19. What are this person's top fears and frustrations? What gets him or her mad or worried?

20. What are this person's top wants and desires? What does he or she want—what is the outcome this person is really after?

If you do none of the previous questions and only answer these last three questions with clarity and certainty, you can use the answers to write an entire book. Consider them your ticket to book freedom.

Getting to the Emotional Core of Your Ideal Reader

Colin Theriot, leader of the website the Cult of Copy, says about writing to your ideal reader, "You should be creating a perceived relationship of trust and reliability and desirability—literally as fast as you can." Colin suggests doing this by making the reader feel like he or she is having a genuine conversation with a real live person, who truly wants to help solve his or her problem.

He says that while a lot of people know what a customer avatar is, they mistakenly think a bunch of demographic descriptions are what make an avatar effective. Instead, "You need to know your prospect's emotional core as it relates to the main problem you are going to promise to solve. You must know what it is like on the *inside* when they suffer and struggle."

Colin believes that this is the part that most marketers skip because they don't know any better. After determining the emotional core of your reader, "You have to craft a corresponding seller persona so that the perceived person making the offer perfectly engages the buyer avatar you are trying to communicate with."

When you do this correctly, Colin states that "the prospect feels like the person making the offer is the right person, with the right deal, at the right time. It's fate, kismet, destiny, etc., that you are meeting. It clicks. The key fits the lock." He goes on to clarify, "Of course, we both *carved* the lock *and* the key. It's not an aligning of the stars. It's just clever marketing magic."

Colin is outlining something I have believed and practiced for years: Solve a problem for your clients, and they will crawl across broken glass to do business with you.

***

When I work with clients, we put all the answers to these questions into a completed Ideal Reader Profile. The Ideal Reader Profile becomes a living, breathing document which may evolve as the book project evolves. Get started on your Ideal Reader Profile right now, before you do anything else. Set a timer and answer the questions in as much detail as possible.

I am including a sample completed Ideal Reader Profile at the end of this chapter. At Book at the Beach, we share it with the writers, editors, graphic design team, marketing and social media teams, potential sponsors, end users, and so forth. Feel free to share it with your employees, business partner(s), or anyone involved in any aspect of the book or business—it will help provide an understanding of your book's goals and direction for them, too.

The profile also provides the added benefit of helping you and your team know where to find the book's ideal reader as you begin to market the book. For example, for my Book at the Beach product, I target quick-start alpha males over forty who have been in business for more than five years or are serial entrepreneurs; they are happily married with children, and often, their wives are involved in some aspect of the business.

The biggest thing getting in the way of them writing their book is not a lack of confidence or shortage of ideas or cash flow: it's *time.* I know they are not often on Facebook, so that is not where I am going to market to them. The best way for me to find my target clients is to go to an event that they are either hosting, attending, or speaking at. I join target-rich environments such as business accelerators, mastermind groups, or business chambers or councils and meet them through word-of-mouth. I know that if I get myself in front of them, more often than not, they will hire me. They have been looking for me, but they don't know it until I am standing in front of them.

Topher Morrison is the Managing Director of Key Person of Influence (KPI) USA. He helps business owners focus on using tangible, proven strategies in order to become a key person of influence in their company, network, or industry. Recently, he sat down to write his latest book and realized he was making a huge mistake.

CASE STUDY: The Importance of Knowing Your Avatar by Topher Morrison

I share with everybody in KPI the importance of always writing with your avatar in mind, and I'm still guilty of not following those instructions. I was working on a paragraph about pitching, and as I reread it, I realized that I had written it without my avatar in mind. *Everybody would benefit from this book*, I thought. As soon as I reread it, I realized it was written for "anyone," and it didn't fit.

I went back to what I preach and I imagined my avatar sitting across a coffee table from me in desperate need of the advice I was about to share. I rewrote the paragraph saying what I needed to say to that one particular person. Here is the before and after to show you how important it is to do that exercise.

BEFORE paragraph:

At some point in time in your life, you'll have an opportunity to pitch an idea to someone. I could argue every day you have this opportunity—be it where to eat with your special someone or what movie to watch—they are a pitch. Need to communicate with your boss why you want a raise or that new computer? That's a pitch. Regardless of whether you're pitching for a million dollars' worth of equity in your business to an investor or something as simple as getting your kids to do their chores, they all share key components to win them to your side.

My avatar is a small business owner in his late thirties, married with one kid, in start-up mode, and needing to get money for the business. If you fit that profile and read that paragraph, would it speak to you? Maybe. Maybe not. Here, it is rewritten to that avatar:

AFTER paragraph:

When pitching to an investor, the future of your business is on the line. You can't risk taking unrehearsed chances or winging it. You need to know that when you stand or sit in front of a group of investors, you are polished, well-rehearsed, and know the answer to every question that might be asked. But, beyond just memorizing your content, you need to be aware of the components that make a successful pitch work. Once you know this, no matter who you pitch to—be it a wealthy investor for millions, your special someone for your movie selection on date night, or your kids for picking up their toys—everything comes down to how you pitch.

In this case study, Topher still said what he needed to say, but he reprioritized the highest importance based upon the avatar. This version had him realize all the other ways pitching would be valuable, versus trying to start with those other ways first, possibly causing him to lose the reader.

Always, before you sit down to write, take thirty seconds to imagine you are sitting across the table from that avatar. Imagine they ask you one specific question about your expertise, then write down that advice. Your book will be far better than if you just write it for everyone.

Here is a sample completed Ideal Reader Profile. Notice how incredibly specific we get.

SAMPLE: Completed Ideal Reader Profile

Ideal Reader "Malcolm Evers"

Malcolm Evers is a male, fifty years old, living in Tampa, Florida. He is married to Paula, a beautiful woman with blue eyes and brown hair. Malcolm and Paula have two children, one boy (20) and one girl (22), who are both in college.

Malcolm is 5'11" tall with brown hair that he keeps cut short. He is clean-shaven and dresses in jeans or solid pants, business-casual plaid shirts, and steel-toed boots while on the job.

Although Malcolm has an athletic body, he is about twenty pounds overweight. As a successful entrepreneur, Malcolm works hard on his business and does not put any time or effort into maintaining his physique. As a result, Malcolm knows his body no longer feels like it used to. Since turning forty, things began to break through the stress of life for Malcolm. He does work out a couple of times each week and is aware that he needs to be more consistent and make better diet choices.

Malcolm was educated at his State College and runs his own successful business, manufacturing windows for the construction industry. Malcolm is excited these days that the costs of energy are coming down, as it means development is picking up. The construction industry overall has increased an average of 14 percent a year every year for the past three years.

Malcolm earns an annual salary of $300,000 and has real estate investments as well. Malcolm is a fairly savvy investor and owns a few income properties.

Malcolm is a patriotic American. He wishes sometimes that he had gone into the army, but his life did not unfold that way. He supports the troops and respects the veterans. Malcolm regrets the way the country treated Vietnam vets and agrees with the current national posture towards veterans, regardless of the mission they are serving. Malcolm is non-partisan when it comes to his political beliefs.

In college, Malcolm showed leadership potential; he was involved in several extra- curricular clubs and fraternities, in which he learned much about leadership. Malcolm majored in Business and achieved B-grades throughout college.

He is a family man and attends church every other Sunday. Malcolm enjoys the rituals of his life, like going out for a nice dinner every Friday night, but deep down, he is longing to bring more romance into his marriage with Paula. Malcolm feels as though he has put too much time into his work over the past fifteen years and is now feeling ready to focus more on his marriage and enjoying his life.

Malcolm 's wife, Paula, is also employed, working as an executive for a local business in a different industry than Malcolm. Paula's lifestyle is busy, and she has her sights set on retiring in the next two years. Even though her children are still in college, Paula is already anticipating having grandchildren with whom she will spend her time.

Malcolm is a member of his local Chamber of Commerce, although he rarely attends meetings due to his workload.

Malcolm makes the most of his time on the weekends. He loves being in the outdoors. He enjoys fishing and hunting. He and his wife hire someone to do the house cleaning, the landscaping, and to maintain their property, as they believe their time is very, very valuable. When it comes to their time and deciding how to spend it, Malcolm and Paula use the following formula: they calculate their hourly rate, and if the task falls below that rate, they hire someone to do it. Malcolm and Paula consider this a foolproof way to ensure the highest and best use of their time.

Malcolm enjoys scuba diving, although he has not gone diving in the past few years due to being so busy with his work. They have taken scuba diving trips to very unique places, and Malcolm has experienced catching sailfish and marlin.

Malcolm and Paula have aspirations to visit China, Africa, and South America. Although Malcolm keeps a "bucket list"—a list of all the places he would like to see and things he would like to do—he always prioritizes his business first when it comes to how he spends his time.

Malcolm and Paula agree that their lives would be improved dramatically if they could be more engaged and productive. This might take the form of owning commercial real estate and working part-time, engaging in their work on their own terms. Both Malcolm and Paula do not want to be "chained" to the business day in and day out. They want to have the freedom to choose how much and when to engage in work activities.

Buying History

Malcolm and Paula own an RV. They also live on the water, own a boat, and have some recreational land, although they rarely get to use it. They put a percentage of their earnings into IRAs. However, a sizeable portion of their net worth is invested in their business. They are adventurers at heart, yet calculated risk-takers.

Malcolm and Paula own their home and continue to pay down a mortgage they started during the recession. They sent their two children to private school, although in the early days there were times when they could barely afford this.

Malcolm drives a Ford four-wheel drive truck, a top-of-the-line luxury model. Malcolm enjoys the practicality of the truck, even though he wants to have something that is not commonly driven by many.

Overall, Malcolm is pretty frugal with his spending and is intentional with where and how he spends his money. He does appreciate the finer things and makes sure his family is well taken care of; he's not the type to wear Armani suits. He is more a "salt-of-the-earth" man who is the first person at the warehouse each day. He is very aware of money and spending because he has been managing his business for twelve years. He is entirely aware of all his expenses and holds himself accountable in the process. Malcolm knows that the top line is important, but it's the bottom line that he cares about. He knows that generating a bigger top line through more revenues and production is only one part of running a successful business. He also wants to control his costs. Malcolm wants to personally make more money while also spending less money so he has more with which to invest in his future.

Technographics

Malcolm and Paula have a personal desktop computer for use in their home. Malcolm has an iPhone and does a lot of his emailing from his phone. Malcolm is neither a techno- enthusiast nor a pessimist. His views lie somewhere in the middle: While he loves the convenience of being able to leverage technology on the go, he hates being tied to it, because he always feels compelled to re-engage in his work when he should be relaxing. Malcolm recognizes that technology allows him to be more productive. However, he sees this as both a blessing and a curse.

Paula has a tablet, which Malcolm also enjoys using from time to time. Overall, he spends around two hours a day online.

Malcolm buys many things online—plane tickets and concert tickets, for example. Malcolm uses Google to research ideas and concepts and is resourceful around finding the information he seeks.

Malcolm does not use social media very much at all.

What is bothering Malcolm right now? What is causing him pain?

Malcolm and Paula are throwing everything into their work and are self-professed workaholics. Malcolm and Paula want more time to enjoy their lives, but they are very focused on winning and maintaining their current standard of living. As a result, they are highly focused on work each day. They are acutely aware that having their own business brings freedom but also ties them down because they are solely responsible for their own success or failure. This awareness has led to financial independence and preservation of wealth becoming paramount for Malcolm and Karen.

Malcolm and Paula are smart enough to know that Malcolm's business has value, particularly the warehouse in which the business operates—over twenty thousand square feet of prime industrial real estate.

The issue now is whether or not to continue moving the business forward, a business that now makes $500,000 yearly, or to dispose of the asset in hopes of generating a fair return. They have an idea of what the warehouse is worth, but they have not figured out the best way to manage that asset. Malcolm and Paula agree there is always an element of risk hanging over the head of business owners, whether they acknowledge it or not.

They have both sacrificed a lot over the years. There has been blood, sweat, and tears. And they have seen it all: They have been screwed by customers and vendors but have also had great customers and vendors. They began with nothing, and the business is now worth millions of dollars. Malcolm has really personified "true grit" as he has grown his business.

Malcolm's pain points include the need to protect his wealth, the lack of freedom he feels in his life, and the impact of the recession on his clients.

What are his top fears and frustrations?

The top fear for Malcolm is losing everything he loves and has become accustomed to—his wealth, his wife, his lifestyle, and his life overall. Malcolm finds himself frustrated by unpredictable problems that occur in his business, problems that need to be solved on a frequent basis. For Malcolm, these problems look like supplier disruptions or employee turnover. Although Malcolm does have some loyal employees, he finds that it has been difficult to maintain a continuity of trained, skilled, and reliable people that will treat his business the way he does. He has found it difficult to find someone who would internalize the sense of urgency he feels. He has observed that unless the business is theirs, people will not treat his business the way he does. Malcolm does, however, have a few key staff members around him who share his values, sense of urgency, and importance around the business. He truly has been the captain of his ship and has been rarely questioned by his subordinates.

It is hard for Malcolm to admit, even to himself, that he doesn't know everything about his business. Malcolm also knows there are potential pitfalls and is afraid to make the wrong move.

What gets him mad or gets him worried?

Malcolm is worried lately because a regional firm that also manufactures windows has moved into his local market. This firm bought a facility just a few miles from his own, right after the recession. Because of this increase in local competition, Malcolm has seen prices erode, which he finds frustrating.

What are Malcolm's top wants and desires?

Malcolm thinks he wants more money and to retire. He knows he needs to work out more, but he doesn't. He knows he needs to spend more time honoring his relationship with his wife—making deposits in the "Love

Bank"—but he doesn't. Malcolm fears he is addicted to the success and feels like he can never get enough money. Malcolm doesn't feel safe when it comes to how much money he has.

While money is important to Malcolm, he knows it is only a means to an end. The end is that Malcolm finds his happiness, his peace, and his safety margin that can only be achieved through accumulation and protection of wealth.

Malcolm wants to make the right decision and optimize the outcome of that decision so that he finds himself in a place where he can take a breath, reassess the situation, and become more connected with himself, his wife, and his life.

Ultimately, what Malcolm wants is to embark on the path to self-actualization. However, Malcolm does not *know* this yet. Malcolm thinks he just wants to retire, drive his RV around, and have sex with his wife like they did before they had kids. That's his dream—or so he thinks.

On a deeper level, Malcolm is seeking self-awareness and an inner connection with who he is. He isn't even aware of this desire. This is because he is caught up with trying to "get it all done." Malcolm is not highly evolved when it comes to emotions. He is not in touch with his inner feelings, nor does he know how to explore this or become more evolved in this area. Malcolm is good at his work and is dedicated. Malcolm has achieved the status he currently enjoys because he had a plan and has worked according to that plan.

Even though Malcolm has built an entirely lucrative business, it has put him in a position of scarcity in his mind. Malcolm is concerned with knowing how he will manage his costs in the coming year or how to reposition them. He is always solving problems, but he is still in a scarcity mindset rather than an abundance mindset. Malcolm needs to shift his thinking to that of abundance in order to be able to relax and enjoy his life.

As Malcolm evolves, what he wants is freedom and a financial safety margin, a place where he can truly feel that he has what he needs.

If you are not as specific and detailed as this sample, go back and refine it. Refer to it as often as necessary. As you review your Ideal Reader Profile at later stages, feel free to modify or remove some things that don't fit or are not right. This profile will guide your content choices moving forward. You will know the appropriate language to use, whether it's important to explain a concept, or whether the ideal reader will feel as if you are talking down to them.

I would recommend timing this activity. Allocate ninety minutes to do this (on your own or with a team member, business partner, or employee). If they can type while you speak, even better. Then pass off your answers to an assistant and have them compile it all into a profile like the example I provided.

Chapter 5:

WHAT AM I GOING TO WRITE ABOUT?

You are probably wondering why this step comes *after* determining your ideal reader. I know it may seem counterintuitive. The reason is because your message may vary depending on who you're writing to. Once you have completed your Ideal Reader Profile, the next step is to figure out what, exactly, you want to write about.

Get clear on your message:
- Who are you?
- Why should the reader listen to you or read what you have written?
- What problem do you want to help them with?

If you're looking for writing ideas and you run your own business, a good place to start is by asking your clients.

Think about the following:

- What is the number-one thing clients are always asking you?
- What do you often find yourself repeating?
- What do your clients want to know the most? Information that satisfies an immediate need or impulse should sell well.
- What do you have to contribute that is not already in the marketplace?
- Be alert when people around you complain about something that annoys them, especially concerning your area of expertise or your business. The little— and sometimes big—annoyances of life can be good material to write about and can build your credibility or position you as an expert.
- Be curious about everything. Ask your clients questions. Give them feedback forms. Try to get in their heads. Remember what it feels like or what it felt like to be in their position.

Write something people want. You may think you know what people really want, but have you asked your ideal reader? Have you done your research? Do you have evidence of it? It must meet some specific need that you know they have, without any doubt. Below is one way to know if people are interested in a particular topic.

Write a Post on Your Blog or Website

- Did you get many comments?
- Were they enthusiastic?

- Did you get a lot of social media action (retweets, likes, etc.)?
- Did you get more private emails and direct messages than usual?

There is More Than One Way to Write a Book

One of the easiest ways to write a book is to capture your insights or lessons on a regular basis. One of my clients—we'll call him Scott—shared with me recently that one of the main things he is working on is trying to capture insights. "When you are in a business or have a particular area of expertise, you get a constant flow of insights," he says. "You are being exposed daily, and in some cases hourly or by the minute, to knowledge and information. Unfortunately, when you're in a business, you often become so close to the operation that you overlook very valuable insights and take them for granted."

If you could simply start to capture these insights, scribble them down, or grab your voice recorder and start recording, it wouldn't take long before you had enough content for a book. And it is another way to easily "write" your book without the process being overly disruptive to your life.

Similarly, you can use any existing content you have from the past to write your book. You don't have to reinvent the wheel. Use blog posts, webinars, or podcasts and build your book outward from there. You could also record yourself as if you were coaching a client or speaking to an audience. Get that material transcribed and turn it into a book. You don't even have to do it yourself; someone else can record you, harvest your material, and write your book for you (more on that in Chapter 10).

Refer to the Experts

Who are considered the "experts" in your field? You can use these experts in different ways:

a) Use an expert to back up what you are saying.

b) Build on what an expert says.

c) Disagree with or question the expert: When done properly, disagreeing with an expert opinion can carry great weight and influence for your client. It also helps you to be on top of new information and gives you the opportunity to add any missed information.

Insider Tip: Write to Teach

Ninety-nine percent of the time, when you're writing an e-book to tell your client about something, you're either writing to show them how to do something or you're writing to teach them information they don't have but want badly. To teach something to someone, you have to learn it all over again yourself, as if for the very first time. See your subject with a beginner's eyes, or try and get in the beginner's mind.

Rapid Results Outline

It's time to do your outline. I know, I know. No one likes doing outlines, including me. But I have a hack. I call it the Rapid Results Outline. This is a timed exercise, so it keeps you from overthinking or spending more time than the process truly requires.

This takes less than twenty minutes and will be the best twenty minutes of the entire book process.

> **Bonus resource:**
> For a digital, downloadable version of the Rapid Results Outline, visit my website at
> **www.KarenRowe.com/book-bonus**

RAPID RESULTS OUTLINE

Step 1: You have two minutes to write your title and a one-paragraph description of your business. Do not move to the next step until instructed to do so.

Title:

One-Paragraph Description:

Step 2: You have three minutes to write down sixteen subjects you might write about in your book. Shut off your left brain, meaning don't worry about any details such as grammar and spelling, and shut off your inner critic. Just ignore any passing thoughts or criticisms that may enter your head while you are writing. *Trust your instincts.*

1
2
3
4
5
6
7
8
9
10

11 ....
12 ....
13 ....
14 ....
15 ....
16 ....

Step 3: You have two minutes to reorganize, make improvements, spell check, and arrange the previous sixteen subjects in logical or chronological order. List the new order here:

1 ....
2 ....
3 ....
4 ....
5 ....
6 ....
7 ....
8 ....
9 ....
10 ....
11 ....
12 ....
13 ....
14 ....
15 ....
16 ....

Step 4: You have two minutes to pick your top ten preferred subjects.

1 ....
2 ....
3 ....
4 ....
5 ....
6 ....
7 ....
8 ....
9 ....
10 ....

Step 5: You have seven minutes to write down four topics/issues/pieces/components for each of your top ten categories.

This is your book outline. This should give you a clear picture of your subject matter and message. You also now have forty subjects you can blog about. Each day, choose one of these subjects and write about it.

Insider Tip

One of the reasons the Rapid Results Outline works so well is because it can be a pitfall to return to the previous day's writing, so do not review what you have previously written until all the writing is done and you are ready to edit. Your main goal during these initial phases is simply to get all your ideas down, keep momentum, and complete your outline within a specified time.

Chapter 6:

WRITE YOUR SHITTY
FIRST DRAFT

*"Almost all good writing begins with
terrible first efforts. You need to start
somewhere. Start by getting something
—anything—down on paper."*

—Anne Lamott

Expert Positioning Book Blueprint[2]

Alright, so you've completed your book outline. That will
become the cornerstone of your system—your expert strategy, secrets, or steps that form the bulk of your book. The
following blueprint breaks down the components of your
book even further—chapter by chapter. This is the juice. My
very best secret sauce.

In oversimplified terms, your book can be divided into three parts.

One: The reader will come to the book with a major problem or pain point. (You spend time highlighting this pain point and illustrating that you understand their situation. When done properly, you can even articulate it more clearly and more in-depth than they could.)

Two: You establish why you are the best person to solve this problem (your story of struggle or "earn the right" story).

Three: You solve that problem (your framework or blueprint).

The following is a breakdown of each of these components in greater detail.

INTRODUCTION

The purpose of the introduction and Chapter 1 is to set the context and the need for your book. Then you get more into expert positioning before detailing your system and wrapping up with a conclusion.

1. Define your ideal reader's problem. What are the challenges they are facing? This is the reason *why* for the book.

2. Personally relate to their problem. Tell your (brief!) story of struggle. Demonstrate to them why you are the best person to solve their problem ("I've been there, too.")

Expert Positioning Book Blueprint

Chapter 1	Define the Problem
Chapter 2	Your Story of Struggle
Chapter 3	Outline your Framework (the Solution)
Chapter 4	Step 1 of Solution
Chapter 5	Step 2 of Solution
Chapter 6	Step 3 of Solution
Chapter 7	Step 4 of Solution
Chapter 8	Step 5 of Solution (etc.)
Conclusion:	Call-to-Action/Next Steps

3. Tell your story of finding a solution. Did you interview other experts? Did you discover the solution through your own experience?

4. Your results. Share your "aha!" moment (e.g., "I finally realized [the principles I am going to teach you in this book] and since then, the result I've had is: ....").

5. Your promise. Share with your readers what they're going to be able to achieve as a result of following the strategy outlined in the book. Give them a (big) motivational reason to continue reading.

6. The overview. Finish the introduction by offering a "sneak preview" of what's to come. What are some of the key takeaways they will have after reading your book? You want to build curiosity in your reader and lead them right into Chapter 1.

CHAPTER 1: Define the Problem

1. Rehash the current state of your topic, but this time, get more specific.

2. Refresh the reader on how things have changed—either in your industry or in the personal lives of those who have used your method to overcome their problem. The reader should get excited here about what is possible for them.

3. Give them the bad news—although the industry has changed, or the potential for individuals to change is available, most people don't take advantage of it. They needlessly continue struggling (sad face).

4. Reestablish yourself as an expert—the holder of the solution. Set up the need for them to continue reading.

5. State your new approach—I like to call this "The Way Out."

6. Declare who wins/loses in the world—what has to be done differently for the reader to achieve their goals.

7. Share more of your story at a broad level—reveal more about your struggle than you did in the introduction, and more about how you overcame key obstacles.

CHAPTER 2: Your Story of Struggle

1. Share your story (again). You already shared a brief summary of your struggle and how you overcame it, but this is where we're really going to do "Expert Story Positioning." Talk about your story of struggle *from the beginning day.* If you don't have one, then share the story of struggle of your students or your clients.

2. Lead your story all the way through the solution—this should be a couple of pages. Remember to position yourself as someone the reader will like—no overinflated ego here. Be humble. Be real.

3. Share not only your own successes but the successes of your clients.

CHAPTER 3: Outline Your Framework (the Solution)

1. This chapter will reveal how you are going to solve the reader's problem that you identified in Chapter 1. It is the Big Picture of how your strategy works. The framework is often broken down into a particular number of steps or "secrets." For example, *The 7 Habits of Highly Effective People* or *The Seven Principles for Making Marriage Work*. Organize your content into steps the reader can follow to achieve their goal/ solve their problem. Each step becomes a chapter of the book. You want to stick to an odd-numbered but manageable amount of steps, either three, five, or seven. But no more than seven, or the reader will find it overwhelming.

> It helps to visually demonstrate your solution in a pyramid, concentric circles, or a graphic as I have on page 67.

2. Debunk the naysayers. As soon as you teach some-one the "how to," they go, "Well sure, he can do that, but I can't." Call them out on their shit—yes they *can* do this, and here's why. Teach them how to overcome the key obstacles (time, money, fear, etc.).

CHAPTER 4 AND BEYOND: Solve the Problem

The "bulk" of your book happens in Chapter 4 and continues for as long as it takes to explain each component of your framework. Each chapter is one step/secret/principle, etc.

1. Secret #1: Explain the principle in depth, the action steps, obstacles, etc.
2. Secret #2: Explain the principle in depth, the action steps, obstacles, etc.
3. And so forth.

CONCLUSION

1. Recap your entire book—the length can range from a couple of paragraphs to a page or two.
2. Their one thing. Tell them what their next (first) step is now that they've read the book. You want to leave them with one simple action for them to take so the reader is not overwhelmed with all the information you have just shared.
3. Share a meaningful story—touch the reader's heart with a success story of your own or that of a client.
4. Motivational close: Inspire them to go forth and kick butt (e.g., change the world, quit smoking, write that book).
5. Call to action. This should be "visit my website," "come to my workshop, seminar, or boot camp," or "schedule an initial consultation with me."

Insider Tip

Consider writing five calls to action that you can sprinkle throughout the book to drive readers into your funnel. (This is based on your end in mind and the result of the work you did in Chapter 3. If you have a marketing team or someone who manages your marketing, ask for their contribution for this section. Here are a few examples:

▶ Download my free Blueprint

▶ Sign up for additional training

▶ Visit my website

▶ Consult my coaching call

▶ Watch my video demonstration

▶ Listen to my podcast

▶ Join us on Facebook

▶ Buy a ticket to my event

▶ Watch example presentation(s)

▶ See more information on my mastermind

Etc....

That's your book.

I guarantee you that following this guide will help you write your book ten times faster than using no guide at all.

But don't be mistaken—we're not expecting quality at this point. This is a starting point, nothing more. In fact, it's a relative given that your first draft will suck—and that's okay. Managing your expectations will take some of the pressure off. Anne Lamott is famous for referring to them as your

Shitty First Drafts: "A friend of mine says that the first draft is the down draft—you just get it down. The second draft is the up draft—you fix it up. You try to say what you have to say more accurately. And the third draft is the dental draft, where you check every tooth, to see if it's loose or cramped or decayed, or even, God help us, healthy."

Once you have written a section, don't come back to it again until you have finished the first draft. At the first-draft stage, you do not want to do any editing. It can be a pitfall to keep editing the same section or chapter over and over again. While it may feel like you are making progress, the editing ends up becoming busywork.

It's also important to note that the Expert Positioning Book Blueprint is intended as a starting point. If you've been paying close attention, you may have noticed that my book doesn't follow this Blueprint to the letter. For example, I don't define the problem of the publishing industry (that would normally appear in Chapter 1) until Chapter 13. But you can bet I started with it in Chapter 1 and chose to move it during the editing process because it made more sense there. The blueprint's sole purpose is to help you get your first draft down on paper in record time.

Manage Your Expectations

It's a worst-case scenario for me: My client Lauren is M.I.A. She hasn't submitted her first draft and isn't responding to emails.

No bueno.

I reach out to my friend Melanie who referred me to her to find out what is going on with Lauren. She hops on a call with Lauren and is able to identify a block. Or rather, an error of thinking. The client realizes that she is under the impression that the first draft of her book has to be, in her words, "a lock" (and then the editing becomes a matter of just moving the words around).

Um, no, sweetheart. That's called a final draft.

Melanie tells her no way; send that pile of steaming shit to the editor and let the editor get the structure down. Then you can see what the key components of the book are and rewrite it chapter by chapter to make a whole.

That was the perfect advice.

I see this all the time: People make writing the first draft so much harder than it needs to be. I blame your high school English teacher. You have likely been taught to self-edit as you go. This is great for a 1,000-word document—not so practical for a 50,000-word book. It gets in the way of your writing progress. We have been ingrained to hand in a perfect final copy and get our grade. Time to let go of your perfectionism. A rough draft is just that—rough. Let go of the belief that it has to be perfect before you submit it to your editor.

It's not your job (now) to worry about the end result. We're not there yet.

It's not even your job to have your book all figured out. It's your job to figure out what you want to say. It's your job to barf out all your brilliance onto a piece of paper and let your editing team do the rest. *You are the content; the editor is the context.* The rest will get sorted out with or without your input, I promise you. That's what an editor is for. Trying to "figure it out" interrupts the natural flow of your writing.

It's also your job to keep the project moving along to the next step, and it's my job to make sure you do that (i.e., to make sure you get out of your own way).

Bonus resource:

For a free chapter template to get started on your blueprint, head to **KarenRowe.com/book-bonus**.

Chapter 7:

WHY STORIES ARE GOOD FOR BUSINESS

"Creating a good voice is not about asking them what they want and giving it to them. It's about understanding how people read, and caring about their experience."

—Nicola Morgan

Our words only account for 7 percent of our communication. The other 93 percent is body language and paralinguistic cues such as volume, pitch, range, and speed.[3] However, in a book, you are not standing in front of your ideal reader, and there are no visuals or paralinguistic cues, so you really only have that 7 percent to effectively deliver your message in print. Therefore, to build rapport with your readers, you have to write like you talk. The way you do this is through "voice."

Voice—what a book sounds and feels like—is the glue that holds the words together so that the book feels whole and strong; it holds the reader to the page. If your voice slips, you break the spell that keeps the reader listening.

Voice gives authority. It is not enough for you to be an expert in your subject matter. You must also create an engaging voice that is authoritative, not just because of the information you're communicating but the way you communicate it.

Non-fiction should mimic your natural conversation but with the leisure to edit your words to be more crystalline than they would be if you were speaking. My aim is that the readers understand the message and enjoy reading the book. I edit ruthlessly, "killing my darlings," as William Faulkner would say, if the ego is getting in the way of delivering my message.

Insider Tip

Be prepared to share your best insight and knowledge. Don't skimp out or "save" your best tips or tricks. You want to give all the value you can, because that's the point of a well-written book. You create value for the reader, you build a relationship, and they will naturally want to find out more about you.

> *"The fact of storytelling hints at a fundamental human unease, hints at human imperfection. Where there is perfection, there is no story to tell."*
>
> **—Ben Okri**

If you want your book to be good, you can't be fake. You have to be authentic, or the reader won't care about you or your content; they can smell bullshit from miles away.

Colin Theriot has great insight on this topic. "Some people can't bear to be portrayed as flawed, or capable of mistakes. In a business context, they fear it will lose them clients." The truth is, however, that it's the mistakes that make for an interesting story. "Fuck a story about riches," says Colin. "It has to start in rags. Or even better, have rags in the middle, with riches on either end."

Colin suggests that you highlight what makes you flawed rather than hide it. "Be the one to point it out. Admit it. Own it. Talk about why it is the way it is and how it's going to be better next time. Then deliver on that. It's a million times more believable and rapport-building than just pretending you are the awesomest since forever and never mess up."

In other words, get over yourself. Be real, be raw, be honest, be vulnerable. Tell the story only you can tell. Forget about yourself, forget about how the story makes you look, and think about how it can impact another person and then write about that.

Andrew Priestley, a business leadership coach, speaker, and bestselling author, says that writing a book is a game changer for your business. At the time of this writing, his book, *The Money Chimp*, has been listed in the Top 10 money books in the United Kingdom for six weeks.

When coaching his clients on how to write a book, he emphasizes, "There is no wrong way to write your story. Authenticity trumps professionalism to a reader 100 times out of 100. Don't stress over the language. Don't stress over the tone. Write like you're describing the problem you solved to a good friend. Use contractions. Tell jokes. Cuss a little, if that's your style. Just write."

Always Write to One Person

Crafting an authentic story takes practice, but the best part is—all it requires is that you be yourself. First, think of the person you're the most comfortable being around. The person who makes you feel the most like yourself, the most authentic. The one you can't lie to or bullshit to or grandstand around. Then write to that person. You want the story to feel intimate—you want it to be the same message you'd be delivering if you were talking to your reader face-to-face or sitting across from your closest ally.

You can also discover your authentic voice by writing, re-reading, and cutting the stuff that makes you cringe. The cringing is because you're trying too hard to make yourself look good. Write like you're writing to yourself—don't think about being judged or oversharing. You can always cut out what scares you later, but usually, the most honest, scary parts are the ones the reader most identifies with—and therefore will build rapport.

Humans Are Hardwired to Remember Stories

Whenever we hear a story, we automatically attempt to relate it to one of our existing experiences. That's why metaphors work so well. Our brains get busy searching for a similar experience, and this helps us relate to that same experience of pain, joy, or disgust.

When you're creating something, no matter what it is—a song, a piece of art, a play, a book—you are peeling off a layer of your camouflage. You are wearing your insides on the outside. You are taking what is most deep and vulnerable and sharing it with the world. This can be excruciating, yet I cannot express enough how important it is that you do this. Being vulnerable builds rapport. If people can relate to you, and like you, they are more likely to want to do business with you.

You can use stories everywhere: in presentations, meetings, blog posts, social media, your website. Try telling a story to replace charts, graphs, and facts. My general rule of thumb is that if there is a place in my presentation where people's eyes tend to glaze over —or if I'm boring myself — that's where I need to tell a story. As long as you are able to make the connection between the story and your main point, your message will be more inherently interesting, memorable, and impactful.

It's Not About You

But don't just tell a story for the sake of telling a story. Remember—you already have your clear and well-defined Ideal Reader Profile; make sure you are crafting content that will engage and compel that particular reader.

Your reader will always be asking, "What's in it for me?" As you are writing and/or editing your book, notice how much time you spend talking about yourself and your stories versus how much time you spend connecting that story back to the reader.

The reader wants to get the win for himself—a book that has lessons from your life that the reader can map onto their own lives. It's very easy to get caught up trying to share a personal story of yours and go into so much detail that you lose the reader. Readers are fickle. When they are reading the book, you want them to be saying, "Me too, me too, me too." Tell your story. Just make sure that throughout your story, you are peppering in comments that take it back to their life or business. They will be able to stay engaged and tolerate the selfishness. Make your stories meaningful *to them*.

You Don't Have to Use Your Own Story

If you don't feel you have any relevant personal stories to tell, it's natural to worry about sounding believable with hypothetical stories. The best way to get around this is by using someone else's story. Some people might call these case studies. I call them client stories.

Start by answering these questions:

▶ What was the problem your client experienced?

▶ What was the solution you provided?

▶ What was their result, in story form, that will be meaningful, memorable, and impactful? Get your reader
   emotionally engaged.

For example, as a financial advisor, if you're writing a
book on *The 5 Easiest Ways to Save For Your Retirement*,
use a real-life example of one of your clients and how you
helped him or her. Then tie it back to the reader.

Chapter 8:

WRITING HACKS

> *"The mind is a dutiful servant and will follow*
> *the instructions we give it."*
> **—Zig Ziglar**

I'm somewhere in the middle of my second book, and I am seriously stuck. All of the tools that I regularly use to pull myself up and out of the gutter aren't working.

Visualization? Stopped doing it. Affirmations? Pfft. Meditation? My mind is so up in arms and so, so far away from a peaceful state that I am up until four in the morning tossing, turning, agonizing.

I have a ten-ton weight on my back. I am carrying the book around with me like a shackle. I am trying to carry on with the rest of my life. I am at an aquacise class, lumbering around in the pool, a ghost of myself. I am meeting clients and doing my job, the thought bubble above my head a jumble of swear words and red, angry exclamation points.

Another day goes by. I have a deadline. Time will not stop for me. It will not wait for me to get my shit together. It will not.

Suddenly, I realize with deadening clarity that writer's block is not about a lack of organization, time management, or alarm clocks. It is about *fear*. Ball-twisting, tit-squeezing, suffocating, destructive *fear*. Writing a book is about learning how to harness that fear and channel it effectively into intense, productive focus—how to have it work for you rather than against you. But I don't know how to do that yet.

One more day goes by. Then two. I am waiting for an answer. I am consumed. I am looking at quotes about how courage is strength in the face of fear; I am writing new affirmations about being a talented, competent, and dedicated writer.

Nothing.

Fuck you, stupid quotes!

I am entreating the Ghosts of Writers Past to open a door, throw me a bone, cut open a vein. Something. *Anything.* I am screaming out for help. Someone help me.

And the help finally comes. A friend. A glorious, glorious friend asks me one simple question: "What's your payoff?"

Blink.

She follows with: "What do you get to be right about?"

Blink, blink.

"What is this fear supporting in your belief system?"

Blink. Blink, blink.

I sit there, agape. Silent. Heart beating in my throat. Squirming.

Check, please.

This, my friends, is what they call Resistance.

In his best-selling book, *The War of Art: Break Through the Blocks and Win Your Inner Creative Battles*, Steven Pressfield identifies that resistance is your biggest enemy in the book writing process, and it can show up in many insidious and divisive ways. It can look like self-sabotage, criticism, self-doubt, procrastination, writer's block, and every entrepreneur's favorite, "busyness." *I have no time to write a book.*

The first step is to identify resistance for what it is. And the second step is to take action in spite of it. This chapter outlines my best tips and "mind hacks" that I have used to successfully bypass resistance and trick my mind through to breakthrough results.

Writing Tips and Mind Hacks

Write Right Now

Don't be fooled into thinking you will have more time later or that "some other time" will be better or more perfect. You won't. It won't. Maybe you have a vision of some blissful writers' retreat where you focus on your book and only your book for three straight days or two full weeks. If you need that, then plan it. Right now. Put this book down, go to your calendar, and figure out what you need to do to make that happen. And if you are interested in spending three days with me in New York City, check out my NYC Writers Camp at **www.nycwriterscamp.com**.

I always think I need a good run at it. Entire weekends of writing in my pajamas without a shower and no responsibility, where my creative spirit can roam free. And that's great when I have it, but it's not always possible. Start with what you do have, such as an extra fifteen minutes in the morning. Can you squeeze in forty-five minutes at the lunch hour or an hour on Sunday before bed? Momentum will build, and that is how a book gets written and finished.

Sometimes, I fail. Sometimes, I skip the forty-five minutes at lunch in lieu of a nap or a mental-health meal with a friend. But I try again the next day. And if I fail two times out of five? Well, that's three more days of writing than if I had done nothing at all.

The only time your book ever has a chance of getting written is *right now*. In this moment. That is the creative process in action. The process is getting past one hurdle, cutting a swath through the resistance, and getting your project moving along to the next phase. It's like that old saying, "How do you eat an elephant?" *One bite at a time.*

Start Somewhere

Do something. Take any action you can take, even if it's small. Ask yourself, "What is one action I can take today to carve out time towards writing my book?" Maybe the action is looking at your calendar or having a conversation with your spouse about finding time to get away; maybe it's starting a "Book Fund" or "Writers Retreat" fund or emailing a graphic designer or declaring a publish date on Facebook or buying the domain name of your book.

In Charles Duhigg's famous book, *The Power of Habit*, he talks about the science of creating habits and how changing one aspect of our life can cause an entire series of positive changes as a byproduct. Changing a keystone positive habit (for me, going from not doing any meditation to meditating daily) triggers a domino effect, dissolving other negative habits (drinking too much alcohol, unhealthy food choices, going to bed too late, procrastinating on my book) as well. By making single, small changes to support our lives, we consciously and subconsciously leverage the tiny gains we experience, and our minds form patterns that allow us to see that greater achievements are within our grasp, which we automatically act upon.

Write for Seven Minutes a Day

There is much research that shows that writing for just seven minutes a day can generate astounding results with your writing. I wish I could take credit for this idea, but it's not mine, I just stole it. In my 30-Day Writing Challenge, I encourage my authors to start by writing for seven minutes a day for the first week. Of course, you are free to write for longer, but seven minutes a day is the minimum. Don't edit. Just write.

Generally, it's recommended that you write first thing in the morning or last thing at night. These are some of our most creative times of the day. Believe it or not, lying down when you write stimulates the creative part of the brain. It could explain why many of us get great ideas just as we're drifting off to sleep.

Insider Tip

Keep a voice recorder or your cell phone next to your bed so you can capture those brilliant ideas that come to mind just seconds before you're about to fall asleep. Think you'll remember it in the morning? Think again!

Create a Crisis

Create non-negotiable, external deadlines with somebody else *who will not let you off the hook*—someone who will not buy your shitty excuses. Don't give yourself any wiggle room. I'm convinced this is the only way anything ever gets done, ever. Remember the story I told in Chapter 1 about how I finished my first book? *That deadline saved my life.*

One of my clients—I'll call her Juliette—had a book that was about 40 percent complete. It had been stalled for more than seven months as she got swept up in the day-to-day of running her thriving business, being a wife, being a mom to two small children, and, frankly, the general discouragement she felt from writing her book.

But Juliette did something smart: She gave herself a non-negotiable, external deadline. She finally got fed up enough that she set her book launch date and then *booked the venue*. She put dollars down. She talked to one of her clients who committed to sponsoring her event. And we were off and running. Once she had a commitment to someone other than herself, it was the motivation she needed to get her book over the finish line. In five short weeks, we went from 40 percent to 100 percent complete.

The key is to create a sense of urgency. Nothing has been more effective for getting my work written and published than a non-negotiable, external deadline. In other words, I write and edit my work as if there's a gun to my head.

The first two books I wrote were with a publisher, so there truly was a sense of urgency. While writing my first book with only an eight-week deadline, I discovered that I work extremely well when there is no way I can get out of it. I was given more time for the second book I wrote—about three months—and it wasn't as effective. I took as much time as I was given. And you will use as much time as you give yourself. Give yourself a deadline and honor it.

I create deadlines for myself, with my team, and with my clients. I have set up deadlines right before vacations or when coming up on the holidays or a birthday. If I really want to enjoy my Christmas or my birthday or my vacation, I need to get this done.

Give Yourself an External Reward (or Punishment)

I have heard of authors giving themselves financial incentives, like a reward or a gift—they get to go shopping or buy that latest gadget—for finishing their books.

I have also seen authors give themselves a financial disincentive, such as having to pay $1,000 to a cause they oppose vehemently. A friend of mine set a goal of losing twenty pounds in a certain amount of time, and if he didn't, he would have to write a check to an association he abhors, like Westborough Baptist Church.

There are apps like Write or Die where they have punishment systems if you stop writing. These strategies aren't for everyone, but if they get you results, then great. Figure out what works for you and stick to it.

Treat Yourself Like a Client

Be ferocious about your time. Protect it. Defend it. Bare your teeth. Do not schedule appointments or let other people use the time allocated for your book writing. You would never treat a client like this, so start according yourself the same respect you would give your clients or customers. If you have time scheduled, you cannot skip it. My rule is that if I do not honor the writing time I have scheduled, I have to move it to another time in the day or later in the week. It starts to pile up quickly. And if I don't get to it during the week, I have to spend my weekend making up my lost time. This gets old fast.

I have written in my car with my laptop perched against the steering wheel in between meetings. Is it the ideal, inspiring writing environment? Definitely not, but I have learned to take my writing time wherever I can get it.

Suck It Up

You're tired, you worked your butt off all week, you had networking events all week and social events most of the weekend. By the time you finally sit down to write, you just don't want to do it. You would much rather be watching *Last Week Tonight with John Oliver* or playing with the dog. *This will happen to you more times than not.*

I feel for you. I really do. I've been there, and I have felt your pain. Don't think for a second that we haven't all at one point or another felt the exhaustion and desire to do anything but write the damn book. You can come up with a million excuses why you can't write.

Save your energy and just meet your word count goal. We don't just write when we feel like it, when the inspiration hits us, or when we are bursting with ideas. You write when you are so tired that you fall asleep typing. Stand your ass up and push on until you finish your daily writing goal. Pick one of the chapters in the outline that is the easiest thing for you to write about. Push through. Sometimes, to get things done, you have got to dig deep and do the crap you don't want to do on the days you don't want to do it.

If you don't want to do it, try breaking your word count in half. If that still isn't going to make a difference, ask yourself, what is the minimum acceptable amount of words you can type without completely embarrassing yourself? Is it two hundred words? Fifty words? Seven words? Just do *something*. And then commit to it. Or put the timer on for seven minutes. Write for just seven minutes. And what you'll find is that those fifty words or that seven minutes will turn into four hundred or five hundred words or more . . . and the seven minutes may turn into forty-five.

Am I repeating myself? Good.

Work Quickly—Don't Overthink

The best way I have found to not come to a standstill is to:

    a) Create a project plan

    b) Start with an outline

    c) Follow a framework

    d) Time my writing blocks

These four steps allow me to work quickly, which prevents me from overthinking—which can become a pitfall that slows down or stops the book project altogether.

Use the Pomodoro Technique

The Pomodoro Technique is a time management strategy where you work for twenty-five minutes, then take a five-minute break, and repeat for your entire day. I prefer to work in ninety-minute blocks with fifteen-minute breaks. If I am tired or pressed for time, I will work in forty-five-minute increments. Divide work time consistently with regular breaks.

This technique is based on the idea that frequent breaks can improve mental agility. It's is not about getting more done in less time; it's about distraction-free focus. During this time, you are focusing on writing and nothing else. Your phone is turned off or in airplane mode, you are not checking email or Facebook.

Nor is the technique about spending more time writing; it's about making the time we have count, freeing you up to work on your business, be with your family, or whatever you want to spend your time on. You can feel a sense of accomplishment and make a ton of progress with just forty-five minutes a day.

Tony Schwartz, CEO of The Energy Project, says that most people hold their productivity back by not rigidly scheduling work and rest breaks throughout the day. "We don't push ourselves to maximum output. Instead of 'giving our all' for brief sessions, we distribute our effort throughout the day, leading us back to busywork to fill our time."

What if your entire writing day consisted of two ninety-minute sessions a day? Three hours, and then you could take the rest of the day off? Welcome to my world. The rest of my time is spent running my business, meeting with clients, answering emails, bringing in new business, and networking. And some days, none of the above. Some days, those three or four hours of deliberate practice is all I can manage. And I'm okay with that, because it's probably still more real work than other people's eight-hour work days.

Do the Dirty Work First

Spending time on the hardest tasks allows you to better manage your energy levels. It is known as deliberate practice. Mark Twain is known for his quote, "Eat a live frog first thing in the morning, and nothing worse will happen to you the rest of the day." Eating your frog first thing in the morning simply means, do your hardest or worst task first. For me, that's exercise, but for you, it may be writing. If that's the case, decide how many writing sessions you will have per day and then have them. You will sleep better and be better at managing energy levels if you follow this advice.

> *"There are three things that writers love: praise, money and interruptions."*
>
> **—James Frey**

"Trojan Horse" Your Writing

As I mentioned, I know that I am the most productive in the morning. I work hard in short, focused sessions. I can work quickly and productively and uninterrupted for up to three hours, sometimes up to four hours, until I hit a wall. And before I know it, I'm doing "make-busy" work—checking my social media, answering emails . . . not being productive.

In his TedX talk, "How Better Tech Could Protect Us from Distraction," Tristan Harris tells us that it takes twenty-three minutes on average to refocus after we have been interrupted. Not only that, we also cycle through two different projects before we come back to the original thing we were doing. This is based on a combination of research from

Gloria Mark and Microsoft. The more interruptions we get, the more we create bad habits of self-interruption.

The average person self-interrupts every three and a half minutes. If I need to self-interrupt, my trick is to switch to something else that will move the project forward, like sending a few emails to request testimonials or writing a short list for who I would like to write my book foreword. While it's not technically considered writing or editing, it feels like an escape and is still productive.

Sometimes, I will avert my focus entirely to a different book project. Here's the real trick, though—the Trojan horse part: *When I've had enough of the second project, I'm ready to return back to the first project.* At this point, I've usually forgotten what was bothering me on the first project, and I hit it head-on, right over the hurdle that seemed impossible before. It's like pulling one over on yourself; it's a direct act of subterfuge used to trick your brain against resistance and win the war of writing.

Treat Your Mind Like It's a Five-Year-Old

At any given time, I have anywhere between twelve and seventeen book projects on the go. My goal is to publish one of these books a month. I know that on average it takes me an hour to edit ten pages of a book. I have found great success by breaking down the tasks of a manuscript into ten-page increments. I am goal-oriented, so I like to make a list of the page numbers (Pages 1–10, Pages 11–21,

Pages 22–32, and so on) that I then check *and* cross off at each stage, which I find twice as satisfying.

☑	~~Page 115 - 125~~	1 hour
☑	~~Page 126 - 136~~	55 minutes
☑	~~Page 137 - 147~~	25 minutes
☑	~~Page 148 - 158~~	55 minutes
☐	Page 159 - 169	1 hour, 20 min
☐	Page 170 - 180	40 minutes
☐	Page 181 - 191	35 minutes
☐	Page 192 - 202	45 minutes

SATURDAY 📅

TOTAL: **6.5 hours** 🕐

Tracking my hours also makes it easier for me to feel accomplished at every stage.

That's my big secret.

How I manage to be so productive is by treating my mind like it's a five-year-old and breaking tasks down into such miniscule chunks that it would be embarrassing and ridiculous for me *not* to complete them. Also, I celebrate every single step, no matter how minor.

You don't have to see the whole staircase. Just take the first step. Think about the sheer fierceness of sitting down and facing your resistance and doing it anyway.

And how awful and good it feels.

Don't Stop Writing Every Time You Feel Like It

This is a little tough to master at first. Resist the urge. According to research by Janet Polivy, our brain fears big projects and often fails to commit to long-term goals because we're susceptible to "abandoning ship" at the first sign of distress. Additional research by Kenneth McGraw suggests that we're prone to procrastinating on large projects because we visualize the worst parts—the perfect way to delay getting started.

Set a Timer and Follow It Strictly

When you start working, start your timer. When it goes off, stop wherever you are. You can finish the thought, but don't finish the section. Take the break as scheduled and then come back where you left off. Usually, when the timer goes off, you have worked through any sticky point that made you want to stop, and you are on to something that you *want* to come back to.

Never Come back to a Blank Page

This is my single greatest trick. I guarantee that making this one minor adjustment will keep your momentum going and ultimately improve your longevity as a writer. If you are on a roll, stop writing just before you run out of things to say.

Coming back to a blank page can be demoralizing and can cause you to get stuck. Don't go on writing and writing and writing until you feel like you're finished. If you do, you'll find yourself asking: What's next? Then you get up and walk away from it, and it's hard to rebuild that momentum.

Hemingway said it best: "When you are going good, stop writing." The best part of this technique is that if you stop yourself when the going is good, you can't wait to get back to it because you know what you are going to say next.

These are the very best tips I have on how to get a first draft finished. In the next chapter, we'll discuss tips on how to revise and refine your new creation.

Chapter 9:

DON'T EMBARRASS YOURSELF—TIPS FOR SELF-EDITING

"Effortless writing is the result of great effort."

—William Zinsser

"The better I get at writing, the more often I delete what I've just written."

—Mark Manson

All right, so you've pushed yourself all the way through a first draft. Congratulations! But before you submit your work to an editor, you will want to do some self-editing. There are a number of strategies you can use to save some time and money before you hire a professional—especially if you've just brain-dumped all over the manuscript. Here are some basic tips.

How to Self-Edit Your Book

Walk Away from Your Book

Taking a break is the kindest thing you can do for your writing. Something magical happens when you walk away from your work; the words settle into themselves, and you are able to come to the work with a fresh perspective. Suddenly, you can see what content works and what doesn't.

When you return, approach it from your ideal reader's point of view and as if you'd never read it before. You will notice things that you were too close to the material to be able to discern before. You might notice the thinking isn't linear, your explanations aren't clear enough, entire sections no longer make sense, or you are over-explaining. The voice or tone might feel off.

If possible, give yourself a minimum of a week, preferably two, between writing and editing your manuscript. Build that into your project calendar from the beginning.

Print it Out

Read your book in a form different than the form you wrote it in. If you wrote your book out longhand, read it digitally. If you wrote it on your computer, print it out. Even reading it in a PDF versus a Microsoft Word document can make a difference. Reading it in a different format will allow you to see a ton of mistakes that you didn't notice, even if you've already read that paragraph or that page a hundred times.

Looking at your work in a formatted draft will highlight mistakes that didn't stand out before. What I mean by "formatted draft" is the last version before you send the book to the printer. There might be typos, for example, or paragraphs that are too long or too short. You can get a proof copy before you go to print, once the design has been all done, and that's sometimes the most valuable editing I do.

Reread It in Its Entirety

If your book is a 50,000-word manuscript, rereading the whole thing might not work for you, but I do recommend that you reread the book in its entirety at least once. If you can, just read it for content enjoyment, as if it were for the first time. Rereading can help you clear up any confusion, notice details, and help you gather more information to enhance understanding.

Read It Out Loud

This process always works for me. If I am tripping over words, or if something that sounded good in my head sounds awkward when spoken, I know some wording needs to be fixed. Reading aloud can smooth out the rough edges.

Ask Quality Questions as You're Reading.

- Does it make sense?
- Is it true?
- Is it authentic?
- Does it work?
- Does it advance the conversation?

Have these questions in your head as you're going through your manuscript. If there's a section where you think, "There's something that's not quite right, but I can't put my finger on it," make a note of it and see if your editor can help you with that section. An editor will appreciate your direction, since it gives them a guideline about the areas in which they can be the most useful and supportive.

Do Big-Picture Editing First

By this, I mean structure and content. In other words, ask yourself:

a) Have I said everything I want to say—is all the content here?

b) Is it in the right order?

I strongly suggest *not* doing a line edit (looking at the manuscript line by line, editing every last detail from start to finish). Not only is this extraordinarily time-consuming, but it practically guarantees that you'll never finish your book. You will get stuck in this endless loop of rereading the same sections over and over. It will trap you. And later on, the editor may end up cutting out the content you spent hours reworking, so don't waste your time.

Big-picture editing will be the best use of your time; that means looking for chapters or sections that need to be cut out. They may be too advanced, confusing, or off-topic for your ideal reader. Remember, you have a clear picture of who your ideal reader is and what problem you solve for him or her. Look at the content through the lens of your ideal reader.

Having an ideal reader in mind will help you determine what language to use, what content to include, and what you need to explain. Here is a simple example of language: I often just introduce myself as a writer or a collaborative author. I don't always use the word *ghostwriter* because not everyone knows what a ghostwriter is. Now, I simply explain that I write books for other people and I put their name on it. The person I'm speaking with determines my vocabulary.

Look for Missing Information

Taking a break for a couple of days or weeks is also beneficial because it provides us with the opportunity to remember whether there was additional content we wanted to include but haven't yet. For example, do you need to insert more stories or case studies?

A case study is a straightforward story that clearly outlines a problem, an action, and a result.

1. You had a problem, or your client had a problem. *Example: I have been working on my book for a year, and I can't seem to get it done.*

2. What action did you take, or what action did you guide your client to take?

Example: I hired a ghostwriter to help me manage the project to completion.

3. What was the result? *Example: I published my book.*

In the example above, I have oversimplified and told the story in the most boring possible way to illustrate my point. If you can share it in a compelling way, the reader is going to remember it.

Ask yourself:

- How can I enrich the main points of my message?
- What would make it more interesting or fun?
- What's my best story that illustrates this point?

You can really have fun with this part. (No, really—you can.)

Trust Your Instincts

> *"The most essential gift for a good writer is a built-in, shockproof BS detector. This is the writer's radar, and all good writers have it."*
>
> **—Ernest Hemingway**

You might be sitting there thinking, *Well, I don't think I have Hemingway's radar*, but I promise you, you do. It's just about paying attention.

You'll notice this when you're rereading your work or reading it aloud to somebody else; there will be a little voice saying, "Hmm, that's not quite right," or, "This section doesn't work" or "I love this part." You need to listen to that voice, because if it's not quite right for you, it's not going to be right for the reader.

The same goes for feedback from editors as well. Trust their professional opinion. Trust your instincts, but trust theirs, too. Listen. You know your target reader better than the editor sometimes, but you don't want to force something through for the wrong reason. Ask yourself, "Why am I so attached to this content? Is it about being right, or is it about the integrity of the final book?"

Be Prepared to Cut 10 Percent

My very first editor from the first book I ever wrote always told me to remember that my second draft equals my first draft minus 10 percent. Once you're happy with your work as a whole, it is time to cut. Depending on your confidence level, you can either cut out 10 percent or you can wait for your editor to cut out 10 percent, but you can anticipate that much, at least.

Remember, the first draft is not the time to edit. That is your brain dump; it's where you're putting down everything that you've always wanted to say, without editing, judging, or criticizing. That means that most of us overwrite. We use more words than we need and often weaken our argument and our story in the process.

Look at the word count on your piece and try to cut out 10 percent of the words. If you've written an 800-word blog post, aim to cut it to about 720 words. If you've written a 45,000-word manuscript, you want to cut that down to just over 40,000 words. You particularly want to keep an eye out for things you've said more than once. Unless you're deliberately using repetition as a rhetorical device, it's unnecessary. Trust that your reader is going to understand your message the first time.

Watch for Words That Weaken Your Message

Cut out wishy-washy phrases like "in my opinion," "I think," or "it is my belief that." This is your book. Your name is on it, so we obviously know that these are your opinions and that this is what you believe and think. Saying so weakens and dilutes the statement—and your credibility. Another thing that weakens your message and credibility are words like "actually." The subtext denotes that you are lying or only telling a half-truth.

Show, Don't Tell

Ask any editor, and they will list "telling, not showing," as the single biggest problem they face. This has become a well-worn cliché but is an essential tool in any writer's toolbox.

It is one thing for a writer to understand the problem, but it is another for the solution to be applied consistently. You need to know your "tell" from your "show." Remember what we discussed in Chapter 7, about finding your authentic voice and using story to build rapport with your reader? I started off in Chapter 1 by not only stating my problem as a first-time writer but by creating a compelling and evocative story that took you on my journey. It would have been less compelling if I'd merely said, "I had to write a book and I only had eight weeks to do it."

Run a Spell Check

Honestly, I hope this step makes you laugh. This should go without saying. And yet here I am saying it.

Paying an editor per hour to correct your spelling mistakes is not the best use of their time . . . or your money. You want to be presenting the best possible version of your manuscript, bringing it as far as you can so that your editor can focus on the areas where you may not be as skilled.

These simple, straightforward tips will help you master the art of reaching the desired standard for your work *before* you hire a professional. You don't want to be paying a professional to do the kind of work that you can do. And I'm not even suggesting that you do it personally. If you have an assistant, pay them at their hourly rate (which is less than yours and less than an editor's) to polish it up before you submit it to your professional editor.

Chapter 10

BRING IN THE TROOPS (HIRING PROFESSIONALS)

There's a romanticized idea of writers as solitary creatures, akin to holing themselves up in cabins for days, weeks, or months on end, before churning out their masterpiece, à la Henry David Thoreau. As previously discussed, removing ourselves from other people and earthly needs and stepping inside our private Sensory Deprivation Tank (or Book at the Beach) is sometimes just what we need in order to write. However, once you get that shit down, it's time to bring in the troops.

There Will Be Blood

I'll let you in on a secret: Even a professional writer like me has to wrestle with some demons in order to get my book to the final draft. My inner dialogue sounds something like:

Jesus, Karen, you run a WRITING BUSINESS—how can you not be done with this never-ending book yet? YOU shouldn't have to ask for help. You should have it all figured out. You should HARDLY need any editing at all . . . you are a pro! Why is it taking so EFFING long?

The editing process is going to be boring, hard, and painful at times. There is no bypass for that, I'm afraid. However, placing ridiculous expectations on yourself is the biggest obstacle to finishing a book. Once I acknowledged that I was letting my ego run the show—and realized how unproductive that was—the solution was easy: One, let go, and two, ask for help.

It's hard for me to let people see my writing when it's not perfect. But bringing someone else in can offer a fresh perspective and allow you the opportunity to delegate work you hate and focus on the content you are passionate about, which is what prompted you to want to write a book in the first place.

Editing: Where the Rubber Hits the Road

Editing is the most underappreciated part of book writing. The majority of the effort takes place in the editing. This is where all the heavy lifting takes place. Consider your editor like a makeup artist: they make your writing look *good*. As discussed previously, many people confuse editing with writing. He or she is there to create a final product of which you can be proud, improving your work beyond what you could accomplish on your own.

Insider Tip

Get in community—whatever that looks like to you. Either hire a professional coach, assemble friends, join online membership groups, join mastermind groups, consult business accelerators, or meet up with other authors; anyone who can help you move forward. These options offer accountability and feedback and will improve your writing techniques.

In addition to the aesthetics and mechanics of writing, professional editors are critical for something else—they remove all the parts of your book which are of no interest to anyone else but you. In other words, they edit out the ego. As a writer, you are the generator and creator of the work, and you're very close to it, so it's important to have a second set of eyes on it—a professional who can be objective, provide constructive feedback, and strengthen your work.

Writers can sometimes get frustrated with the editing process, but here's the truth—editing is only a problem if you make it a problem. An editor's job is to make your book better. And sometimes that involves adding content, moving it around, or removing it entirely. You can't take it personally. It doesn't mean you're a "bad writer" or that you shouldn't continue writing, and it definitely doesn't mean that you shouldn't publish your book. If you can accept this as part of the process, take the edits in stride, and not view them as criticism, then inevitably, you will get to the end of the process with a book you are proud to call your own.

Hiring the Right Editor

You don't want to hire just any editor. You want to hire the right editor for you.

I want someone who will raise the bar on my work—to verify and check facts, names, and dates, work on spelling and sentence structure, and improve the readability of my work. It's a relief to have someone else handling those critical pieces—someone who knows when to take the comma out and when to leave it in.

On that note, be aware that editors will defer to the rules outlined in a given manual of style. *The Chicago Manual of Style* and American Psychological Association (APA) style are the two most common. Authors in Canada and Europe are more likely to use APA, while America is more likely to use *The Chicago Manual of Style*. When you hire an editor, ask them if they have a style sheet so you will know what to expect and can have a conversation with them.

There are multiple different types of editors, but the four main categories are developmental editors, substantive editors, copy editors, and proofreaders.

Developmental Editors

Developmental editors develop a project from initial concept to draft. They can consult with you before writing begins, and they can help plan the organizational features of your writing project.

Developmental editors can support you with clear structure from the beginning and will help you come up with a plan. They may write and rewrite text, conduct research, or offer topic suggestions. If you already know that you're not great organizationally and you need some help ordering and structuring your thoughts, then a developmental editor is great for you. Once you have that structure or an outline (which is one good thing high school English did for us), then you can unleash and focus on what you have to say. Turn off that internal editor and critic and just get to the writing.

Substantive Editors

A substantive editor will work with you once you have a full initial draft. They help bring your first draft to its final format. They might reorder content or rewrite segments to improve the readability, clarity, or accuracy. This is also known as big-picture editing.

Copy Editors

This is when your draft is nearly final. The copy editor reads each sentence carefully and fixes all the errors. They are the ones who are detail-oriented, fastidious, and analytical. They edit for spelling and punctuation, capitalization and grammar, awkward phrasing, and fact verification—and they do it all while still preserving the meaning and voice of your text. At the copyediting and proofreading phases, editors do not make substantive (or content) changes.

Proofreaders

This is the absolute final stage. A book is proofread after the interior layout has been formatted, after all the photos, graphics, or visual elements have been added, and you're about to send it to print. Proofreaders correct errors that may have been overlooked during copyediting or introduced during the design process. They might do cross-checking or typesetting.

When it comes to hiring an editor, you may find that you only need one kind, if you know what your strengths are. For example, I have a talent for big-picture editing and developmental content. I know I can get my manuscript—and yours—to a certain stage before I, too, need to bring someone in. If you happen to be analytical and love grammar and editing, then focus on that. Perhaps you are a great planner or have a strength in high-level content development, meaning you might not need a developmental editor. Identifying your strengths, finding the right editor for your project, and knowing what to expect will make this process more effective for all involved.

What to Expect from an Editor

Once you know which type of editor you need, the next step is to make sure the individual you select has a work style that jives with your own. In my case, the editor is as much a part of each of my books as I am. I typically work with the same editor and have for years because I know we work well together. The more projects we do together, the stronger our working relationship.

The writer-editor relationship is a collaboration. Talk with them from the beginning about how you see their level of contribution and involvement, and see if they feel the same way. They may not. The clearer you are about your expectations with your editor, the better and clearer the final product will be. The more you communicate with them, the more likely your editor will be able to deliver exactly what you need and to do so quickly and accurately.

Expect editing to be a process. It may include two or three rounds, back and forth with your editor, as you progress from a developmental or substantive edit to a copyedit and, finally, to a proofread.

Understand that the first draft is really a roadmap to the final product. Be prepared for the final draft to be dramatically different from the first. Welcome the changes. Use the first draft as a touchstone and remember that it's a creative process. Be open to your editor's suggestions.

Remember: Editors are on your side. They are there to strengthen your work and make you look good. Keeping that role in mind is one of the keys to maintaining a success-ful relationship with your editor.

How Much is Editing Going to Cost?

When it comes to editorial fees, rates for editors vary. Make sure you are clear on payment agreements from the start. Some editors charge by the word, some by the page, some by the project, and some by the hour. I prefer to charge by the project and negotiate a flat rate for editing because I sincerely dislike tracking my hours. I find it a distraction, and I tend to forget to do it. Secondly, I don't want my clients to be worried about the quality of their book because they fear the price will go up. I want them to focus on their content, not on tracking hours or dollars.

That being said, I've known editors who are extremely efficient and can get more done in two hours than others might in eight, so I wouldn't freak out if they charge by the hour. No matter how they charge, ask them why they do this and listen to their response. In my experience, most will have a good reason for charging the way they do. And if you are dissatisfied with their answer, find a different editor.

The longer the edit, the less they should be charging per word. I've known editors who charge anywhere from two cents a word up to as much as five or six cents per word. Rates per hour vary based on experience but can range from $25 to as much as $75 or $100/hour. If the editor has a specialized knowledge or skill set, his or her rate will be higher. For example, I've paid up to $75 per hour for a book about industrial real estate that required an experienced editor with real estate knowledge. Rates can be in the $80 to $100/hour range if they, say, have a PhD in English Literature or an MA or an MFA.

If you're looking at a full-length manuscript, budget approximately $1,500 for one round of quality editing of a roughly 30,000-word manuscript. You can expect to pay up to $6,000—again, depending on length and number of edit cycles. If you're looking to cut costs, remember that you do get what you pay for. For the most current editing rates, a good resource is the Editorial Freelancers Association at www.the-efa.org.

Hiring a Ghostwriter

Here is the beauty of working with a ghostwriter: *It's all of the glory, none of the work.* As I have mentioned, the average book takes in the neighborhood of four hundred hours to write. A good ghostwriter may be able to reduce your time investment to around forty to sixty hours.

Picture this. You meet with your ghostwriter, brainstorm your book idea and content, and record your audio (say . . . at the beach . . . over the course of three days). It feels like a natural conversation. Then you go back to your life. Weekly, you get an email from your ghostwriter with a list of tasks they have completed while you were running your business.

There may be a small list of items for you to complete. But you're trained now to record the audio yourself, and you speak those points of missing content into your phone and send the audio. It takes you about thirty minutes a week.

And that's as complicated as it ever gets. Sure, you will have to review and approve the final content, but if the ghostwriter is in charge of the structure, the outline, and making your content sound good, then your time is focused on helping fill in missing content and reviewing the work done, rather than slaving away over multiple versions of each book.

Sounds great, right? It is.

Is Ghostwriting Considered Cheating?

I get asked this a lot. Many people feel that it's just "not right" or doesn't feel good to have someone else doing all the work. But this isn't the way I see it. I'm not writing the book for you and slapping your name on it. I am collaborating with you to take your knowledge and expertise and put it in a format that creates an organized, captivating, and marketable book. The book will use your exact words, as told to me via hours of recorded interviews.

My clients are already so busy and successful that finding the focused time required to sit down and write on a regular basis is a near impossibility. If they don't hire me, their book will not get written. And this has nothing to do with talent or ideas or even their ability to write. This has to do with delegating tasks to the right people so they can focus on their genius, which is the best use of their time.

How Can You Write a Book for Me and Make Me Sound Like Me?

For my process, I get to know my clients first. I build a relationship with them. My first session is spent getting clear and specific about who their ideal reader is, so that we can get inside their head and write directly to them. We also determine the preferred voice and tone to use with the manuscript, and the client has the ability to make adjustments before signing off.

Just like hiring an editor, you want to conduct an evaluation process to make sure that you choose the right ghostwriter for you. Here are some factors to consider and questions you can ask when making your choice:

Experience

- How many books have you written?
- How long have you been a writer?
- What is your training? Any college or university degrees?
- Are you a native English speaker?
- Do you have a portfolio I can see, and will you allow access to previous books published?
- Have you published any of your own books?

Pricing

- What is your fee structure?
- What is included in the package or rate? What is included in your fee? (For example, is the fee solely to produce a manuscript, or does the fee include other services, such as publishing my book for me? Are print copies or only digital copies included?)
- Are there hidden fees or penalties for not meeting deadlines?

Scope

- What is the deliverable? What is the word count promised?
- Is there anything that isn't included?
- Are there additional costs outside the scope of this project? If so, what are they? These costs may include:
    - ▷ Book publication
    - ▷ Book distribution
    - ▷ Marketing and public relations
    - ▷ Travelling and accommodation
- Will I retain all rights to the work?
- Do you have a confidentiality/non-disclosure/non-compete clause?
- Are you working on other projects with the same subject matter that will conflict with this book?
- Do you have an interest in the subject matter?

- What is your availability—when can you start? How many hours per week or per month can you dedicate to my project?
- Will you be able to work in tandem with my deadline?
- How do you prefer to communicate—phone, email, text?
- How often can I expect to hear from you/receive an update?

Finally, ask yourself, do you like them? I can't tell you how much smoother a project goes when I *enjoy* the team I am working with. Don't underestimate the importance of hiring someone who complements your work style, jells with your (or your team's) personality, and aligns with your company or book's vision and purpose.

What to Expect When Working with a Ghostwriter

When determining what you are willing to pay for a ghostwriter and how long the process will take, it's important to note that every ghostwriter writes at his or her own pace (which is why I charge by the project and not by the hour). Remember that statistics show that, on average, a book takes in the neighborhood of 400 hours to write—and the writing is only a portion of the work that gets completed.

Before a ghostwriter types the first word of your book, he or she will spend a number of hours with you planning your book. I also spend a great deal of time communicating with my clients via phone and email, conducting interviews, researching, editing, rewriting, and—depending on the scope of the project—perhaps working with other vendors such as proofreaders, interior designers, and cover artists. This adds many more hours of work to the project, and I pay any vendors with whom I work. This all gets worked into my project fee.

The Million-Dollar Question: How Much Does a Ghostwriter Charge?

First, you have to understand what you are paying for. Ghostwriters are essentially giving up *all* of their rights to the book; they are doing the hard work, and they are allowing you to put your name on it. That is going to cost you something. Most people have no idea how much work is involved in writing a book or what each contractor will charge for various editorial and design phases.

Ghostwriters for celebrities, former presidents, and athletes get upwards of $60,000 to $80,000 a book; some of them can charge as much as $120,000. It's not uncommon to negotiate a fee for service and, in some cases, a royalty agreement or, in very rare cases, a percentage of the book advance.

Tony Schwartz, the ghostwriter of Donald Trump's 1987 memoir *The Art of the Deal* negotiated a joint byline, meaning his name appears on the cover. He received half of the book's $500,000 advance and half of the royalties. We know from an article in *The New Yorker* that "the book was a phenomenal success, spending forty-eight weeks on the *Times* best-seller list, thirteen of them at No. 1. More than a million copies have been bought, generating several million dollars in royalties."

Don't worry, you won't have to pay this much. For the rest of us who may not have the cash flow or platform yet to pay those sorts of fees, you can expect to pay more experienced ghostwriters in the neighborhood of $15,000 to $30,000 a book, or more for those writers really in demand. In general, charging a flat fee rather than hourly rates works best for these types of projects. My rates are based on two things. One, how much of the work you are willing to do versus how much of the work you want us to do, and two, how quickly you want the book done.

Insider Tip

Don't hire a ghostwriter for less than $5,000. You can find ghostwriters through online job sites who will work for incredibly low fees, but beware—you get what you pay for.

WRITING AND PUBLISHING OVERVIEW

As I mentioned, most people have no idea how much work is involved in the book- writing and publishing process. Here is an overview to give you an idea of the various stages involved; you may use this guide to negotiate what is included in your editor and/or ghostwriter's services and fees.

Phase I: Content Development/Project Management (i.e., the writing)

Phase II: Editing (three rounds)

Phase III: Design

  ▷ Interior Layout

  ▷ Cover Page

Phase IV: Publication

The following is an overview of my Book Action Plan and what my process looks like.

BOOK ACTION PLAN

Phase I: Content Development (Dates)
Deliverable: Completion of first draft

$..................../month (Estimate based on number of weeks required to deliver the project)

Includes:

• Content Development Sessions

• Consulting

• Revision

• Project Management:

  ▷ Weekly check-in, Status sessions, Publication Concept Projections

Initial Draft submitted for initial edit: ....(date)

Phase II: Editing (Dates)

ROUND 1: STRUCTURAL EDITING

$................. **(Amount based on # of words)**

A full review of the organization, presentation, and sentence structure of your book to ensure clarity and flow of text.

Suggested improvements might include:

- *Recommendations for adjusting the format used to present the material*
- *Recommendations to reorder some of the material*
- *Identifying information that may need citations and/ or permissions*
- *Identifying ambiguities, inconsistencies, or contradictions within the text*
- *Recommendations for rewording and restructuring sentences to clarify meaning and enhance flow*

Initial Draft submitted for client review: (Insert date)

Client to review initial draft: (Insert dates)

ROUND 2: EDIT (DATES)

$................. **(Amount based on word length)**

Editing will include a full review of the organization, presentation, and sentence structure of the book to ensure clarity and flow of text with attention to the following:

- *Correcting faulty spelling, grammar, and punctuation*
- *Correcting incorrect usage (such as **can** for **may**)*
- *Checking specific cross-references (for example, "As Table 14-6 shows. . . .")*

- *Ensuring consistency in spelling, hyphenation, numerals, fonts, and capitalization*
- *Checking for proper sequencing (such as alphabetical order) in lists and other displayed material*
- *Flagging inappropriate figures of speech*
- *Ensuring that key terms are handled consistently and that vocabulary lists and the index contain all the terms that meet criteria specified by the publisher*
- *Ensuring that previews, summaries, and end-of-chapter questions reflect content*
- *Enforcing consistent style and tone in a multi-author manuscript*
- *Changing passive voice to active voice, if requested*
- *Flagging ambiguous or incorrect statements*

Second Draft submitted for client review: (Insert Dates)

Client to review second draft: (Insert Dates)

ROUND 3: COPYEDIT (INSERT DATES)

$.............. **(Amount based on word count)**

A third and final copyedit after the author makes the recommended changes. The editor will review changes that were made based on the recommendations in the initial and second round of edits.

Final Draft Review & Revision (Insert date)

Final draft submitted to client for review & approval (Insert date)

Phase III: Interior Layout (Insert dates)
Formatting of inside pages: for both print & digital

Layout Design—Format Interior Pages of Book

Each Package Includes:

- *First chapter provided with two different formatting options (two different designs; client chooses the preferred chapter look and feel)*
- *Up to three images (photos/graphics)*
- *Headers, footers*
- *Page numbers*
- *Optional: Call-out boxes every three to six pages (where appropriate)*
- *Ready for self-publishing*
- *High-resolution images and/or graphic selection*
- *Final product delivered as a ready-to-print PDF file*

Additionally, ALL content is counted in word count (e.g., table of contents, copyright pages, reference pages, etc.)

Book Cover Design

Each Book Cover Design Package Includes:

- 3 design concepts (client chooses the preferred cover design)
- 2 rounds of revisions to chosen concept
- 1 purchased image (photos/illustrations)*
- Final product delivered as a ready-to-print PDF file

Phase IV: Final Book Development & Digital Publication

$...................

- Convert to ePub or .mobi. Makes your book available on all other digital platforms: iBooks Store, Sony, Barnes & Noble Nook, etc.
- Assign ISBN
- Upload to CreateSpace or IngramSpark
- Files issues and review process

Total Project Estimate Based on Current Considerations: $......................

Estimated Project Completion Date: ....
Launch Date: ....

Whether you decide to hire a ghostwriter, a project manager, an editor or a combination of all three, make sure you are getting the help you need, however that looks for you. Hiring the right professionals will make your contribution easier and help keep the book on track right through to publishing.

> If you are ready to take the next step, visit **www.KarenRowe.com** to set up an initial consultation.

Chapter 11:

SECRETS TO A GREAT BOOK TITLE

A few years ago, one of my clients was convinced she had the perfect title for her book. It had come to her in a dream. It was a great title, and it was very catchy, but in the end, it didn't speak to the problem that her ideal reader needed her to solve. It would have ended up putting her in a service that she didn't want to be in—one-on-one coaching—rather than her true love of teaching workshops. But she was adamant about the name and couldn't let it go. When she realized that the name wasn't going to work, she was so heartbroken that she walked away from her book for six months and had to re-strategize her manuscript and delete most of the content.

When a client comes to me before we've ever started writing a book and says, "I have the perfect title for a book,"

I often ask if they are willing to change that title if it means selling more books. If they say yes, I'll work with them. If they say no, I can't help them because they will be writing a book for nothing. No one will pick up the book or read it.

Having a working title as a place to start is a great idea, but the kiss of death is being too attached to it. Do yourself a favor and be open to the best possible title. You can be 99 percent sure that the title will change. It doesn't matter what you think or what I think; it matters what your target reader thinks.

Book titling is the most important part of the entire book-writing process and one that often gets overlooked. To gain insider knowledge on choosing a title, I interviewed professional Namer (yes, that's really a thing!) Canon Wing. For over two decades, Canon has named products that have earned billions worldwide for clients such as Hershey, Kia, and Best Buy.

"Titling a book is storytelling," Canon shared. "You need to tell a story in order to have a great name." As I shared earlier in this book, storytelling is the best way to engage an audience; as humans, we are hardwired to remember stories. Canon believes that a name, or title, "is the world's greatest, shortest story." And who is the star of the story? Your ideal reader.

Canon continued, "The title of the book should make the reader feel good about themselves. They should feel like the hero of the story."

One of the best—and cheapest—forms of marketing is referral, or word-of-mouth. We want our readers to be proud to share their discovery—your book—with their friends and family. To accomplish this feat, Canon puts potential titles through a four-step test. She looks for the following four attractants:

1. **Emotions.** What is the emotion that you want to promise in your book? You should be able to name the emotion elicited by the title of your book. What you are attempting to evoke should be clear to you and to the reader.

2. **Wish fulfilled.** What is the promise you want to make to your ideal reader? What is the conflict they need to solve? When you're naming your book, you should not be fulfilling your own agenda. You should be trying to say out loud the secret that's pressing on the heart of the person you're trying to serve—the thing that they could scream out loud if they were brave enough. If you say it out loud for them, then they follow you. This is how revolutions are started.

3. **Memorable.** You want a title that sticks in your reader's head. They need to be able to easily recall the name when telling friends or colleagues about it.

4. **New but familiar.** If the title includes vocabulary that is very new and we don't understand what you're talking about, we're going to be confused. We're not going to buy it. If it's very familiar, however, it will sound boring or cliché. You have to find a really good

balance between new and familiar in order to con-
quer this step.

A book title that hits all four of these criteria is *The 4-Hour
Workweek*. It strikes an emotional chord, because who
wouldn't love a four-hour workweek? It screams liberation.
It also is a perfect example of a wish fulfilled; ideal readers
are sitting in their cubicles for forty hours a week, thinking,
How do I get out of here? When they see a book called *The
4-Hour Workweek*, they have to buy it. The title is also memorable because it's short and alliterative. Finally, it's new but
familiar. We all are familiar with the forty-hour workweek, but
the concept of a four-hour workweek is something new and
exciting. We're intrigued, and we want to know more.

In most cases, however, it's a tall order to meet all four
steps in a two or three-word title. Therefore, you have two
choices. You can hit the bullseye, which means it passes all
four criteria, or you can hit one in particular so hard that it
eclipses all the others: It's *really* emotional. Your title could
be so emotionally compelling that it's strong enough to ride
on its own.

Where to Begin

You might be saying, "Okay, Karen, I understand I need a
killer book title. I know what targets I need to hit, but how do
I even get started?! I've got nothing!"

I love Canon's strategy, and I frequently use it as a start-ing point with my book titles. What I often say is, "You'll know it when you hear it." But first, you may know what it's *not* before you know what it *is*. Here is a four-step strategy that I recommend.

1. Brainstorm

There are two parts to a title: the hook and the deliverable. The hook is the sizzle; the deliverable is the steak. Write a list of possible titles. There are no bad ideas at this stage.

Keep the following in mind: What are the benefits of what you do? People don't buy features, they buy benefits. What benefit will your ideal reader get from having his or her prob-lem solved? Common examples include more money, more intimacy, more power, more freedom, more self-expression.

Next, go through your list and ask yourself, regarding each one, "Does it meet those four criteria? Is it emotional? Is it a wish fulfilled? Is it memorable? Is it new and familiar?"

Cross off any title that does not meet all four criteria (or strongly hit the emotional mark).

2. Ask Your Ideal Reader

Share your list with people who are in your target market. Can you create a survey using social media, or can you ask for feedback from your email list? People love to be asked their opinions and feel part of the process—doing this en-gages your audience more and may even make them more likely to invest in your book once it's out.

3. Practice Saying It to People

Take your top-ranked titles and share them with individuals or with an audience who may or may not be in your target market. If they look confused, you haven't hit your mark yet. Does it make sense to people who don't know you or don't know what you do? Is it easy to pronounce? Is it easy to remember?

4. Ask Yourself

Finally, for each remaining title, answer honestly, "Is it for my reader or for me?" Anything that is for you is removed from the list. Anything for your ideal reader, the secret pressing on the heart, is a title that stays on the list until you get the final name. You'll be miles ahead of most people if you just do this one thing.

When reviewing your book title list, remember that no one wants to work. We all want a miracle cure for losing weight or for a better marriage or to get rich quick, but rarely do we want to do the work to achieve it. Don't give your book a title that emphasizes or emotionally reminds the reader of the amount of work he or she needs to do.

Using Canon's technique as a starting point, I have named dozens of books in the two years since I completed her naming course. Take my client Jeff as an example. He is a legend in the internet marketing space, and left the game for a few years because he had been so disgusted by the seedier sales tactics of some of his fellow internet market- ers. He had gotten rich in his niche, but he was sick to death of people asking him how to make money online but not following through with the actions necessary to make that money. He came to me with a working title so preposterous that I can't even put it in print. But I will, just to prove my point. He wanted to call his book *Stop Being a P*ssy.*

Now. Anyone who knows me will know that *I loved this title.* I laughed for days. I would much rather have a title that offends—that will elicit a reaction and wake people up—than a tepid, mediocre, and completely ordinary title. Not only will people remember the title, they are more likely to buy the book. But . . . something wasn't quite right. And Jeff knew it, too. Every internet marketer we know would have absolutely loved that title. But that was not his market. (You see what I mean about not getting too attached to a catchy title?)

After running him through the system I just outlined, we came up with a second title: *Internet Peep Show: Profit Online Without Selling Your Soul.* It was important for Jeff to illustrate that it was possible to get rich, still be ethical, and not end up miserable and alone. While that title was a closer fit, Jeff still didn't feel we had hit the bullseye. His ideal reader would not like that subtitle because they would not care about their souls; they just wanted to make crap tons of money, and make it fast. While his title did illustrate that, it was likely to attract broke, desperate men just looking to make a buck who had no interest in being ethical or doing any real work.

In the end, he chose a title much more appropriate for his ideal reader, in a language that would speak to them: *Money Rehab: Kick the Habits that Keep You Broke.*

Titling a book is not an exact science, and it takes some trial and error. But when you come across the right book title, you will know it.

> **Bonus resource:**
> Still feeling stuck? Gain access to a naming cheat sheet by visiting **www.karenrowe.com/book-bonus**.

Chapter 12:

BOOK COVERS THAT CONVERT

Question: What is the number one purpose of a book cover?
Answer: To sell a book.

Seems obvious, right? You would be surprised how many people still think that book covers don't matter. They do. Next to the title, the cover is probably the most important part of the book. You can write the *best* book on the planet, but if the cover is ugly or appears unprofessional, no one will pick it up, let alone buy it. And if they're looking online, they'll keep scrolling. There are a specific set of rules for cover design that, if not followed, could seriously impact your bottom line.

To put it bluntly, the odds are that you and I are the least-qualified people to determine what is going to sell a book. I am not an expert marketer, and in most cases, I am not my ideal reader. My book cover needs to target people who meet the demographics of my ideal reader. Graphic designers are trained specifically to create a book cover that sells to your desired market.

I wanted to speak with an expert, so I went to the best: Gabriel Aluisy, founder of Shake Creative, a branding and design agency. He is the author of *Moving Targets: Creating Engaging Brands in an On-Demand World.* Gabe's work has won awards and generated millions of dollars of revenue for his clients. Gabe shared which elements make for a book cover that converts:

1. Clear title

2. Simple image explaining what the book is about

3. Visible author's name (even on a small icon)

To achieve these three elements, Gabe uses the following guideline:

Clean, Colorful

The best covers are clean, not distracting, bright, and colorful. The ones that pop out on a bookstore or online shelf are the ones that have vibrant color. With the advent of online stores such as Amazon, iTunes, and Google Play, you're on a virtual shelf with several other thumbnail images. If the cover is not clear, crisp, and to the point, it will get lost.

Use a Sans Serif Font

If you're not familiar with the jargon, a "sans serif" font simply means that the letters don't have edges on the tops and sides. They are cleaner in terms of modern design. Helvetica and Arial are two well-known sans serif fonts. Arial doesn't necessarily make for a great book cover font, but it illustrates what a sans serif font is.

Condense the Font

Reducing the space between letters makes it easier to shrink a word and add more letters to your book cover. When people are viewing it on an online store, they need to be able to read the book title, which might be only twenty-five pixels or a really small image on their computer.

With the rise in demand for e-books, it's more important now than ever to have a clean and compelling cover. It used to be that prospective book buyers would walk into a retail store and pick up a book; if the cover design caught their eye, they'd flip it over and read the back cover synopsis, the author bio, and perhaps some testimonials. Gabe explained, "Amazon does have the feature where you can virtually flip over the front cover, but it still is just not the same as holding the book in your hands. With your book cover being on a screen with twenty-five to thirty other books, there's no personal interaction, no physical touch. You can't zoom in on it with your own eyes, turn it over, or flip through the pages as you would in real life."

A book also has less time to capture people's attention now. Our audience is fickle; they are scrolling quickly on their phones, with their attention divided. Gabe agreed, "We are definitely living in an on-demand world. Readers want to go right for something they are interested in, and they want to get immediate satisfaction. If they don't get in, then they just move on."

With that said, he still considers the back cover an important component of book design. "There are still a fair amount of books in traditional bookstores, and since, even digitally, the consumer has the ability to flip electronic versions of the book to read the back cover, it's still your prime real estate and traditionally the primary way to sell the book."

Typically, there are eight items we want to include on a back cover:

1. Book Synopsis (What is the book about? The problem you will solve):

In *Warehouse Veteran: A Tactical Field Guide to Industrial Real Estate*, John B. Jackson shows you.... [insert solution].

2. Bullet list of the reader's main takeaways:

In this book, [your name] will show you how to: (or you will learn how to):

- One
- Two
- Three

3. What the reader will take away from reading this book:

At the end of this book, you will have.... [insert outcome].

4. Testimonial (Optional)

"[Your name] is the greatest person I've ever met, and you should read this book because. . . ."

—Raving Fan, ABC Company

5. About the Author

Brief three to four sentences. Your full author bio will be found on the last page of the book.

6. Your Headshot Photo

Optional. You can choose to include it on the last page of the book instead. Gabe feels this is prime real estate that should be used to sell the book, not sell yourself. Rather than including a small picture of the author on the back of the book, it has become more standard to include it on the back page of the book along with the author bio. My recommendation is to only put a picture on the back cover if you are a recognizable figure or plan on being one (i.e., you are building a large platform or becoming a bigger brand). This is a matter of personal preference.

7. ISBN and Barcode

You will need a separate ISBN for each version of the book you publish. If you have a print version, it will need a different ISBN from the Kindle version, from the .mobi, from the PDF, etc.

In **Canada**, you can get your ISBNs at no charge at the Library and Archives Canada.

In the **United States**, you must purchase your ISBNs. There are a number of places you can purchase them; do a Google Search and go with the cheapest option. Here are a couple of sites to get you started:

- www.isbn-us.com
- www.bowker.com/products/ISBN-US.html

You are better off getting your ISBNs in bulk (usually sold in a pack of ten), especially if you are considering publishing several books in the future. Each country has different rules around ISBNs, so make sure you verify this information.

8. Publisher Logo

If you self-publish, this will be your company's logo or one you make up.

I use this exact formula for the back cover of my book.

Insider Tip

Include a call to action on your back cover. This should be a short statement that engages people immediately and gets them excited to start flipping through the book. For example, "Turn to Chapter 3 for my secret tip on x," or "My best advice on x can be found on page 123."

If you are thinking of using a picture of yourself on the front cover, don't do it! Unless you're Oprah or Dr. Phil or Dr. Oz., stay away from it.

It's cheesy, and your audience may not know who you are, which may turn them off. Let's be honest— we all wish we had a face that could move books, but let's not delude ourselves.

What to Expect from Your Cover Designer

Generally, designers will run through a questionnaire with you and ask a specific set of questions about who is going to be reading the book. A really good designer should get into the psyche of the target demographic. For instance, Gabriel and his team, who designed this book cover, knew that this book was written for male entrepreneurs age forty and over, and he wanted the cover to have an edgy and "in your face" feel to it. If the book were written for Millennials, on the other hand, the design might have taken a more slick or sleek approach.

Gabe shared, "Marketing professionals know that certain colors are associated with particular emotions." For example, the color orange is associated with change or renewal, so if you're writing a self-help book, orange would captivate that audience. "The designer should think through everything from the font choice to the color palette to the imagery on top of the book."

To be sure that you're hiring a professional designer, ask for examples of their work and look at their portfolio. A good designer should have experience with various types of target markets. They should also have significant technical expertise; there are specific requirements for book cover design that your average author or amateur designer is likely unaware of. For example, a publisher is generally going to ask for a file that is at least 300 DPI, which is jargon for how clear the image is. There are particular regulations for the spine as well. The spine dimension is dependent on the length of your book; if designed unprofessionally, the text on the spine may peek onto the front or back cover.

Finally, make sure that they have experience with cover design specifically for publishing. It's not just about designing the work and delivering it in a PDF; they also have to provide you with a template—appropriate for multiple platforms—for when it comes time to publish.

Help Your Designer Out—Be A Low-Maintenance Date

Once you've hired a designer, send him or her the Ideal Reader Profile that you created in Chapter 4. If you really want to look like you know what you're doing, I am including a copy of the questionnaire I use with all my clients; fill it out and send it to your designer with your Ideal Reader Profile:

Author Design Questionnaire

Title:
Subtitle:
Author:
Publish date:

Book launch date:

Binding type: (make a choice between paperback or hardcover)

Trim Size: (standard non-fiction paperback book dimensions are 5" x 7")

Interior color: (black and white, or do you have color images or text?)

Interior paper: (you have a choice between white or cream)

Laminate type: (options include matte or glossy)

Answer the following:

- Would you like to use black and white or color imagery within the body of the book?

- Do you have any favorite e-book or traditional books that have a "look and feel" you like? Attach an email with book cover jpegs.

- What emotion would you like a reader to immediately feel when they see your cover?

- What do you want your personal brand to be known for? Please provide at least three adjectives (e.g., trustworthy, modern, elegant, honest, etc.)

- Anything else the designer should know with regards to how you'd like the final book to appear?

Note that it will likely take at least three rounds of revision to get to a final product. You can expect to pay between

$350 to $1,000 on the low to mid-range and $2,000 on the high end for a professional book cover. Make sure that your expectations for the cover design are realistic given the price point. If you want a custom cover, then expect to pay accordingly. If you are paying under $1,000, you will be getting stock photographs and not custom design work.

Designers are full of creative ideas, but they are not mind readers. They can take a crack at options for you, but be as specific as possible with your input and feedback. For example, a statement like, "I want a cover that excites, interests, and makes the heart beat a bit faster upon viewing," could mean many different things to different people. The designer would have too many options and simply be taking a stab in the dark.

To help them, provide clear direction. They need to understand you, your style, who you are, what your book is trying to say to your readers, and, most importantly, your ideal reader.

The more information you can give your designer, the more likely they are to be able to deliver the cover design you envisioned. Provide them with as much guidance as possible to better hit the mark!

For Crying out Loud, Get a Current, Professional Headshot

Maybe you've been here: You walk into a networking event or business meeting expecting to meet someone for the first time only to . . . walk right past them, because they look nothing at all like their profile photo! It doesn't just happen in online dating. I know plenty of people in my industry who have been guilty of using photos that were ten years old . . . or forty pounds ago or half-a-head of hair ago. This is one of my biggest pet peeves in the business and author world.

If you lie in your profile photo, your clients and customers might wonder, what else are you hiding? And why should I do business with you or read your book if you're already misleading me?

If you are going to publish a book, you need to have a current, professional headshot. You think it doesn't matter, but it does. I asked Michael McCoy, the executive headshot photographer at MP Studios Tampa, to explain why this is of significant importance to authors.

Michael said, "It only takes one-tenth of a second to assess a profile picture and have people decide whether or not they trust you, want to work for you, or want to know what you have to say." People are making split-second decisions. Authors want to establish themselves as experts and credible people; you don't want it to be on account of your headshot that people don't find you credible and trustworthy.

Michael keeps it real: "You're not fooling anybody. Everybody's getting older at the same rate. Some people put on some weight, and some people lose it. It's just the way that life works. Whether or not you've gained weight, lost weight, gotten gray hair, any of that stuff, it's not really important.

What's important is that if you go to meet with, say a publisher, and the headshot you sent with your bio looks like a completely different person, then it's going to say something about what you're saying in your book."

Michael says that conveying confidence and approachability through your headshot are two of the key factors that you want to get across. A good headshot photographer will know how to draw out your confidence—it doesn't have to be a full smile, and it doesn't have to be fake. Your approachability will show through your genuine smile, through your eyes, and through the emotional response the photographer is able to bring out in you. To achieve this, you need to make eye contact; looking through the lens and at the photographer is one of the most important things to establish connection, trust, confidence, and approachability.

Tips for a Great Headshot

1. Have a professional headshot done. None of that cropping a drunken holiday snapshot or a wedding photo. Don't hold up a selfie. You have access to professionals who know what they're doing and can teach you how to look like a professional in front of the camera.

2. For women, think about the amount of makeup that you put on. Professional headshots don't need a lot of makeup. People think they're going out on stage with lighting blasting at them. But photographers are going to retouch those photos, not to completely change your appearance but to get rid of the stuff that you normally cover up with makeup.

That is a lot easier for them to do if you don't cake a bunch of makeup on there.

3. Trust the photographer. When you find a photographer whose work you really love, be coachable for them when you're in front of the camera. Let them guide you. They are professionals who have put the time and energy into learning their trade.

4. Make sure the photographer you choose specializes in headshot photography. You don't want somebody who does senior portraits, weddings, products, all of that, *and* headshots. You want somebody who is dedicated to headshots, who took the time to learn this one thing and learn it very, very well.

5. Be sure to convey to the photographer what your book is about. Your image should be congruent with the message of your book. You might wear a suit if you are doing a finance or real estate book, for example. If you are a relationship coach, you may focus on a fun, friendly facial expression.

The headshot on your book will, for all intents and purposes, be on the book for the rest of eternity. You might as well invest in a photo that you can use not only for your book but for press releases and in multiple other marketing capacities.

When you're considering your budget, Michael suggests you consider how much your personal brand is worth. How much do you think *you* are worth? That amount will be reflected in the quality of the image you present. Get an image that's killer for the back of your book. Don't be afraid to pay for it, because you'll get a return on the investment.

Chapter 13:

THE FINISH LINE— PRINTING AND PUBLISHING

This step can be confusing, but in truth, it is the most straightforward part of the entire book-writing process, once you have all the information. If you are already working with a ghostwriter, an editor, or a full-service writing firm, they may also offer publishing services. "Publishing" can often just mean printing, (i.e., Getting a digital or physical copy into the hands of your readers) and sometimes the two terms are used interchangeably.

There are two key decisions to make here:

1. Will you publish with a publisher, or will you self-publish?

2. If you self-publish, should you print in bulk or use print-on-demand?

Should I Self-Publish or Publish with a Publisher?

Recently, a client reached out to me with the following question:

> *"I have an editor friend who is encouraging me to find a publisher versus self-publishing. I want to open this book up to all possibilities, and I want to know what you think."*

I can't tell you how many times I get this question. It is probably the number one question I get asked by my clients.

Here was my response:

Focus on finishing the book. Period. Chances are, you are suffering from bright, shiny object syndrome, and finding a publisher will be one more thing that delays getting your book to market and into the hands of the people who need to read it. You will spend as much time trying to find a publisher as you will just self-publishing the damn thing.

Times have changed in the publishing world, and the power of the publishing houses has switched to the hands of the authors. I spoke with a woman recently who has published five books with HarperCollins and came to me to help her self-publish her next book because HarperCollins hasn't done that much to support and promote her. She said it just wasn't worth it.

While publishers are likely to get you on some radio and TV programs and potentially offer you PR opportunities you couldn't get without them, the bottom line is, it's really up to you to make sure that your book reaches all the people who you know will love it. Steven Pressfield wrote, "Here's the deal: Some publishers rock n' roll, while others are rock bottom. And even if you're with a rock 'n roll star of a publisher, your 'baby'—your book—is just one of hundreds of books your publisher is raising. You gave your publisher custody, but there's still some major co-parenting to be done."

There has never been a better time to be a self-published author.

Why It's a Great Time to Self-Publish

In the early 1980s and 1990s, the only real route to publishing and marketing a book was through a traditional publishing house. Being a professional author was a very prestigious club that you were lucky to be a part of; you had to be invited in through well-guarded doors. You not only had to have a literary agent, but you had to have one who was incredibly well-connected. The agent's job was to get your book or book proposal looked at by an editor and convince them to publish it, plus offer strong marketing support.

You have likely heard at least one horror story about an indie author who spent $20,000 to bypass the publishing house gatekeepers and self-publish their book, only to end up with piles of unsold books gathering dust in the garage. But self-publishing has risen above this old joke. The shift to digital publishing blew the doors off the entire author industry.

Amazon, in particular, has transferred the power of the publishing house into the hands of the author. No longer do we need to bow at the feet of the mainstream publishers; we now have access to worldwide printing and distribution with a few online clicks.

Goodbye, penniless writer stereotype. Hello, profitable business.

Today's Book Market

Despite popular opinion, people do still read, and indie titles now account for 58 percent of Amazon.com book sales, taking roughly 40 percent of all royalties. The best thing that Amazon and other online platforms have done is to level the playing field. As far as the average buyer browsing the online shelves is concerned, your book looks exactly the same as one that was published by any of the big publishing houses (as long as you took my advice and got a professionally designed cover). Only industry insiders can tell the difference—it is the great equalizer for authors. In other words, you and I are on the same platform as major publishers. Self-publishing is the very best method available today for getting your book out to the masses

According to Horace Dediu, an industry analyst, as of 2014, Amazon had over 200 million active accounts (and therefore credit cards) on file. Apple had 800 million active accounts.[4] What does that mean? It means that if you self-publish through those two platforms, over one *billion* people can buy your book with just one click. And the best part is, you don't have to deal with any of the day-to-day tasks of processing payments. And instant global delivery is the cherry on top.

The Benefits of E-Books

The book market has been in a tumult since digital reading arrived, but overall, the changes have been hugely beneficial for most facets of the industry (except for indie bookstores, but now, even they are fighting back). More and more, large publishers are looking to successful indies for fresh content and new talent. Thanks to the ability to carry a library in their pockets via e-readers like the Kindle, iPad, and cell phones, readers are more voracious than ever.

The advantage of e-books, from an author's standpoint, is that you can make changes to your book in an instant. If you find misspellings or need to update some information, you don't have to spend hundreds or thousands of dollars on a new print run. In addition, you can make more money by selling a book digitally for $2.99, in most cases, than you could by selling a print book through a traditional publisher for $24.99. If you go through a traditional publisher, you are lucky to get paid nickels and dimes for every sale.

The latest statistics show that Amazon is growing at 119 percent a year, and a recent study reported that digital sales now make up 21 percent of the total revenue at Simon & Schuster, one of the largest book publishers on Earth. Consumers can purchase a print version online, but more and more readers are ordering e-books.

Self-Publishing Is Especially Good for the Entrepreneur Because. . . .

You're a Better Marketer

I'm going to let you in on a little secret: traditional publishers forgot how to market twenty years ago. Their only claim to fame was that they could get you into bookstores. Well, that bookstore now is Amazon.

Self-published authors are making it big because they know that the real money to be made from being a published author is not in the number of books sold but in how that book can be leveraged to grow their business. This is where traditional publishers fall short: They are only interested in selling more books. You are interested in how to make your book work for you.

Although you do have to conduct your own marketing for your self-published book, Amazon has made it easier for readers to find your book online. Amazon has the largest buyer search engine in the world. We would all love to rank number one on Google's search engine, but for an author, in many ways, it's even better to have high rankings in Amazon. Why? Because when people go to Amazon to search, they're looking to *buy*.

It's Faster

Traditional publishers can take up to two years to publish your book. For the fast-moving entrepreneur who gets bored easily, they find this timeline quite painful.

My most successful clients are the ones who understand that the value of a book is in the back end. What do you want the book to do for you? Build credibility? Open doors for TV, podcasting, and speaking opportunities? The faster you get your book out there, the sooner you can start using it to grow your list and attract more of your ideal clients.

There has never been a better time to write a book to build and grow your business, your expertise, and your credibility. I never used to take such a hard stance on this, but recently, I've realized how much this dilemma gets in the way of people getting their books out. The longer you delay, the fewer people you are going to reach, and the longer they have to wait to receive your message.

With so many new and exciting options available for indies, now is the time to innovate, both as a business and as an author. Fresh content is being produced at an unheard-of rate, and readers constantly devour it in their hunt for the next big thing. The chance to *be* that next big thing is getting better all the time, thanks to the modern tendency to want to share anything and everything through social media and word of mouth. Outside the structure of the publishing houses, creators are freer to experiment and to be championed for doing so. That's why innovation is rife at the moment, and the next few decades of publishing are going to be very interesting indeed.

No time for handholding; it's time to rock 'n roll. Tough love. Get your book out. As fast as you can.

What About Printing the Book?

You have two options when it comes to printing: bulk versus print-on-demand. In general, it costs less to print in bulk, but you pay the costs up-front. The more book copies you order, the less it costs per book. Print-on-demand is almost twice the price of bulk printing, but you are paying for the convenience of not having to manage the distribution.

Let's say you choose bulk printing and get 1,000 books shipped to your home, office, or warehouse. Every time someone orders a book, you (or one of your staff) will have to put that book in an envelope and mail it to the customer. You will have to manage the payment (and associated fees for taking online payments). Sure, you earn more per book, but you will have to decide whether you want to deal with the hassle of mailing out books every time you get an order. Plus, if you only sell 150 copies, you still have 850 copies gathering dust in your garage. Hardcover books are twice the price to print versus a paperback, so these are all factors to consider before you start.

Bulk orders are a good idea if you are a speaker or trainer or have a large platform already developed, where you have hands-on access to a large group of people. If not, print-on-demand is the way to go, and I recommend it the most often.

Hiring a Publisher

If you don't have a traditional publishing contract, a subsidy or "vanity" press is an option for authors who don't want to take the time to figure out the self-publishing process for themselves. Services and fees vary widely, and caution needs to be taken that you, as a first-time author (and your wallet) are not taken advantage of.

Although you can shave time off your publishing timeline by opting for a subsidy press, be careful that they don't steal your rights—traditional publishers earn your book's rights because they are investing financially in your book; subsidy presses earn money up front on the publication of your book, so they should not be asking for your rights as well.

> **Insider Tip**
>
> 1. Make sure your text is copy-edited before you send it out for formatting. It is expensive and time-consuming to change text later.
>
> 2. Gather all the documents into one file.
>
> 3. Give it a clear title. Book name + author name + date.

In the following pages, you'll find a handy checklist for preparing your book for the self-publishing process.

Self-Published Book Checklist

Before you send your book to the printer, review this guide to make sure you have included all the elements you wish to include and that you have them in the correct order. *Note: You do not need all of these items.*

- ☐ Book Title
- ☐ Cover Page
- ☐ Testimonials
- ☐ Copyright Page
- ☐ Dedication
- ☐ Table of Contents (formatter will manage this; gets done last)
- ☐ Acknowledgements (can go at the front or back of book)
- ☐ Foreword (written by someone other than the author to lend credibility)
- ☐ Preface (usually used to speak of the genesis, purpose, limitations, and scope of the book; what this book is, what it isn't, how to use it/read it)
- ☐ Introduction
- ☐ YOUR CONTENT! (Also known as the book block)
- ☐ About the Author Page
- ☐ Call to Action
- ☐ Success Stories
- ☐ Back Cover Text
- ☐ Author Bio

☐ Headshot
☐ ISBN/Barcode
☐ Pagination/Formatting IS LAST

Media for Authors: A Few Words on Publicity

"You don't go on TV to sell books; you write books to go on TV."

—Steve Siebold

Your book is published and available for sale. Take some time to celebrate this huge milestone; bask in the glow of being able to hold your baby in your hands for the very first time. Smells sweet, doesn't it?

Now get back to work.

If you've followed my advice from Chapter 3, you started this whole thing with the end in mind. You shouldn't be asking yourself, *Now what?* Rather, you should have a clear and concise marketing plan that illustrates how you're going to pass that baby around (you should already have been sending "save the dates").

First of all, let's get the bad news out of the way. You are not going to make any money on your book. I hate to be the one to break it to you. Remember, the money is in how you leverage the book to work for you. It can lead to paid speaking engagements, increased visibility and credibility, and more clients.

How do you get those speaking engagements and new clients? Through publicity. I interviewed Bruce Serbin, who has secured coverage for his clients in top media around the world. Bruce began his career writing anchor scripts for the evening news and planning story coverage. He utilizes his media experience to better serve the needs of his publicity clientele.

The biggest complaint Bruce hears about hiring a publicist is that it is expensive and there are no guarantees. That is true. He also hears from a lot of authors who tell him their publisher did a lousy job promoting the book and that they don't know where to start when it comes to generating media coverage on their own.

I asked Bruce: "How can you, as an author, be known as the go-to expert in their field? How can you build a map to credibility and be featured by print, online, and broadcast media outlets?" Bruce shared, "By far, the biggest mistake most authors make is thinking that doing a media campaign will equate to books sold. Just because you have a book published, it does not mean you are going to be on the *New York Times* bestseller list. And it certainly doesn't mean you are going to sell millions and millions of books. Maybe if you are a recognizable name or a celebrity, you might, but the average person will not sell that many."

Bruce worked with one of his clients, for instance, for more than a year. They have done a cross-country media tour together, including approximately thirty morning television segments. At last count, he had sold twenty-two books in the preceding month. That's right. Twenty-two. Bruce reiterates, "The reason to do a media campaign around your book is for the credibility factor that only the media can deliver."

Media Campaigns

In truth, you never have to stop marketing your book. Unless the content has become irrelevant or outdated or eventually contradicts with your brand, you can keep handing it out and keep it listed on Amazon and other platforms for as long as you like. However, the book's success in the first few months after launch sets the foundation for its future success.

For a typical author, a two or three-month run is a standard duration for the book's initial media campaign. Although you should have been promoting your book to your newsletter subscribers, social media followers, and so on well in advance of your launch, Bruce recommends not approaching media personnel until you have a hard copy in hand. What often happens is the journalist or producer will say, "Well, can you send me a copy?" If you don't have a copy of that book to send, their perspective is, "What's the point?"

In terms of working with the media, here are some of Bruce's tips for best practices.

1. Understand How the Media Works

I've seen many unfortunate incidents where people had great stories, but they lost a media deal because they didn't know what they were doing. For instance, you never want to pick up the phone and call a TV newsroom at five or six o'clock in the evening, right when they are about to go on the air. They will hang up on you, without even giving you the time of day.

2. Know How to Write for the Media

What a lot of people don't realize—if you look at written broadcast media—is that it's written at a third-grade level. Some of my clients will send me pitches loaded with jargon and language that nobody could understand. You're not going to get on TV like that. Keep your pitch very conversational, relaxed, and laid back, and make it enticing. Get their attention.

3. Always Be Pitching the Media

This is not the kind of thing where you develop a single pitch, send it out, and sit there and wait for the phone to ring. You've got to be pitching constantly. That's how we keep a campaign alive, by pitching angle after angle after angle, coming up with new ideas.

4. Be Ready for Rejection

I get rejected all the time. If you're not getting rejected from producers and editors, you're not pitching enough. More rejection is going to lead to more success, so keep pitching, keep coming up with new ideas and new angles, and just don't get discouraged.

Go into your book writing journey with your eyes wide open: Media appearances do not equal book sales.

If you walk away from my book with only one thing, I want you to understand how important it is to have a strong platform and to have a clear marketing plan in order to promote your book. Writing the book is only one part of its success.

Bonus Chapter:

WRITING A GREAT FOREWORD

A foreword (not "forward" or "foreward") is a short introduction to a book written by someone other than the author, usually an industry leader, expert, celebrity or a person of influence to lend credibility and authority to the book. A great foreword is the icing on the cake that will set your book apart from others. If you are writing a book to establish credibility and propel your business forward, you will want to include a foreword so you can leverage their celebrity to your benefit.

A foreword doesn't contribute any additional information about the subject matter but serves as a means of validating why the book was written and why you should read it. The main purpose of a foreword is to boost book sales. It's a way to introduce someone who may not be well-known.

Approaching Someone to Write Your Foreword

When a person of influence has agreed to write the foreword for your book, you want to make it as easy as possible for them to help you. Write the foreword for them and include the following email template. Presume that you are speaking to their gatekeepers. I have used this template successfully in the past. You would be surprised how many times your foreword gets returned, signed exactly as you wrote it—not because they don't care, but because they trust you. You have made it easy for them.

Foreword Template

Subject: Book Foreword/[Name of person, e.g., Dr. Oz; Colin Powell; Former President Clinton]

To accommodate the very busy schedule of the .... [insert title, e.g., president, doctor, etc.) we have written a foreword on his behalf.

Of course he is free to write his own or edit this piece; whatever makes it easiest for him to participate.

Kind regards,
(Your name)

###

Possible copy:
[Insert foreword]

Insider Tip

Include your foreword right in the body of the email and not as an attachment. (Remember: you want to be a low-maintenance date.)

Six Easy Steps to a Great Foreword

If you are writing the foreword on behalf of someone else, here are some key factors to consider. A foreword does not have to be wordy. Aim for the 1,000-word mark or one to three pages. Make the foreword all about the book and its relevance or benefit to the reader. Share the influential person's expertise *as it relates* to your book. The foreword should give the reader a glimpse into how the book can help him or her and why reading it is vitally important.

Here is a guide for how a key person of influence might write a foreword for you (you can use it as a guide if you're writing it, too).

1. Write about a chapter in the book, the book as a whole, or the author's work in general. Get a copy of the manuscript. If you have the time and the interest, read it. If not, skim the table of contents and read a chapter that captures your attention.

2. Write a short anecdote about something that happened in your life that relates—even loosely—to the book. You can also write something that relates to the chapter you just read.

3. Don't be modest. You are writing the foreword because of your credibility and expertise; now is the time to use it. Don't hesitate to remind people why you are well known in the first place.

4. Say something about the author. Have you met? How long have you known each other (or known *of* each other)? Can you relate a personal anecdote about the author? You could discuss how the author's work has affected your life or the importance of the work you're introducing.

5. If you don't know the author personally, devote more space to the book's message. Talk about the relevance of the book or project and rave about how much you believe in its validity.

6. Wrap it up. If you really want to look like a pro, reference an idea from your opening paragraph again at the end and bring the foreword full circle.

The tone of a foreword should be friendly, chatty, personal, and relatable. End the foreword with your name, title, the title of a recent book you have written, and the city where you live. For example:

Karen Rowe

Founder of Front Rowe Seat

#1 International Bestselling Author & Co-author of

Mass Influence: The Habits of the Highly Influential

Tampa, FL

Conclusion: Version Done is Better Than Version None

"Risk is the perfect environment for miracles."

—Dr. John Garcia

There you have it. I have given you everything you need to get your book done *now*. If I can write a book in three days, so can you.

If you're still hemming and hawing, *stop it*. The fear isn't going to go away. Sometimes, you're going to have to do it afraid. What's the worst that can happen? You could not finish it, that's true. But if you're not trying, or you've never even started, you are already failing. So you've got nothing to lose. Really.

Every writer (and every person) I know has experienced moments of intense failure. But that is what makes you a better writer. Failure is very important; it introduces you to an idea or feeling that you don't ever want to return to.

Done is Better Than Perfect

Many people have claimed authorship of the quote "Version done is better than version none." Whether it was Tanner Larsson or Vinnie Fisher or someone else, I thank you. Because this context will have a big hand in seeing you over the finish line.

I hear it all the time: "*I'm not a good writer.*" I'm going to let you in on a secret: I don't think anybody is a good writer. Good writing doesn't come naturally, although most people seem to think it does. But I know if you're reading this that you are passionate about your business, your subject matter, your area of expertise. Your genius will get transformed in the editing process with a little elbow grease and a lot of tenacity.

As a perfectionist, I can tell you that perfectionism and the writing process are not friends. Because we like to have everything 100 percent right and have it look and be a certain way, we are perpetually disappointed. Very rarely does anything turn out perfectly. And when it does, it has often taken so much time and energy and was so exhausting that it's very seldom worth it.

Your book will never feel done. The only cure for my perfectionism is to move at a speed where I can't overanalyze or overthink. The faster I move, the more imperfect things are, but the more quickly they get done.

For about a decade, the perfectionist in me created someone who never went after anything. Of course, the irony is that I therefore failed at everything just by not trying.

I learned to lean into discomfort. I tried things, and sometimes, I failed miserably, but the victory was in having tried in the first place. You can hire a coach or ask people for advice, but unless you have your failures to bring to the table, they've got nothing to work with. Your results simply won't satisfy.

Take a look at your writing. Whether it's a book or a blog post, are you stalling the process? Is it because you have to feel it's perfect before you let anyone else see it? Chances are you will never feel like any draft is a "lock." Like, ever. So just get over it and press Send. Your editors (and family members and friends and probably your pet) will thank you. Anything is better than nothing. And creating something from nothing is the hardest part. From there, we can reorder, restructure, slash, burn, rewrite, add, delete, cry, triumph and rejoice, and move it along to the next damn step. And that is all that matters in the early drafts of book writing, in running your business, in getting anything done, ever.

Your Time is Now

You now have all the tools you need to make your book a reality. And you've made it this far. The first thing you need to do, now that you've read this book, is kick-start your writing by completing the Rapid Results Outline in Chapter 5. My intention for this book was for it to be the kick in the pants you need to stop holding off on finishing your book.

Embrace your destiny and finally become a published author.

> If you are ready to take the next step, and you already know that you need help, visit **KarenRowe.com/book-bonus** for access to all my free resources or to book an initial consultation with me.

About the Author

Karen Rowe is the owner of Front Rowe Seat, a full-service writing firm. She is an expert in nonfiction and can help you position yourself as a leading authority in your niche. Through her proven system, "Book at the Beach," she is known for helping elite, alpha-male business owners get their books written in three days or less. Her clients include an actor, a retired FBI agent, a reality TV star, entrepreneurs with online empires, and some of the top self-help leaders in the industry. Her passion is to capture genius on the page, and her mission is to help you find your voice and uncover your own unique and powerful story to create an instant connection with your marketplace.

She is the author of *For the Love of Chocolate* and *For the Love of Coffee*—both critical components that have kept her going through long writing sessions—and is a #1 International Bestselling author of *Mass Influence: The Habits of the Highly Influential*, which she co-authored with Teresa de Grosbois.

Originally from Calgary, Alberta, Canada, Karen now lives in Tampa, Florida. She enjoys yoga, sailing, biking, beaching and traveling.

Notes

[1] http://www.sparringmind.com/productivity-science/

[2] Adapted from Brendon Burchard's Total Product Blueprint "Create Anything Framework" http://www.succeedspeaking.com/1257/create-anything-outline-for-information-products

[3] Pretty, Jacqui. *Book Blueprint: How Any Entrepreneur Can Write an Awesome Book.* Grammar Factory.

[4] http://www.businessinsider.com/credit-cards-on-file-apple-vs-amazon-2014-4

CPSIA information can be obtained
at www.ICGtesting.com
Printed in the USA
FSOW03n2132110217
30605FS

9 780986 763861